Scrapbooking

Scrapbooking

An inspirational guide to how to personalize and embellish your own scrapbooks

Oceana

AN OCEANA BOOK

This book is produced by
Quantum Publishing Ltd.
6 Blundell Street
London N7 9BH

This edition printed 2006

ISBN-10: 1-84573-232-4
ISBN-13: 978-1-84573-232-5

QUMS225

Manufactured in Singapore by
Pica Digital Pte. Ltd.
Printed in Singapore by
Star Standard Industries Pte Ltd

Contents

Introduction

Personal mementos need not mean clutter, and in this book we show you how to create twenty-four of your own beautiful albums with easy-to-follow guides.

As in the friendship journals popular with the Victorians, which contained sentiments and thoughts from the heart, locks of hair, drawings of nature, and recorded hopes, the passage of time can be documented and archived for future reference. Birth, death, marriage, and our children's growing up are all integral parts of our existence. Photographs are the most obvious way of preserving many of our memories, but what about those other items that can evoke the same nostalgia and provide hours of fun and interest in their compilation?

Theater tickets, buttons, coins, cards, scraps of wrapping paper, and pressed flowers; all remind us of special dates and memorable places. Often these treasured possessions are left to gather dust on a shelf or sit in a dark attic in an old shoebox, undiscovered until it is time to move or redecorate the room. By then, time has often caused them to deteriorate and what is left is barely worth retaining. At the bottom of a drawer, these cherished items may be a pleasure to find in years to come, but they do not have the advantage of being cataloged, organized, and beautifully displayed.

In this book we show you exactly how to arrange and compose special books and albums that will capture the imagination for generations to come. With the highly original and creative projects, ranging from the basic and simple to the more involved and elaborate, we describe and illustrate how to utilize a range of craft techniques, such as cross stitch, ribbonwork, and collage to touch on just a few. We show you easily achieved and effective decorative devices, including deckle-edging, rubber stamping, stenciling, and embossing, methods of making covers, and general layout and design principles. There is a list of essential materials and equipment for such tasks as cutting and glueing, punching, and pressing. An undemanding and straightforward guide to photograph management takes you through the dos and don'ts of selection, cropping, montage, photo transfer, and

LEFT: *Collect twigs and leaves and recycle an old suede jacket to make a soft, supple cover for your album.*

laminating and mounting for the ultimate storage of your forever-safe archive.

With handcrafted designs and clear step-by-step instructions, we demonstrate how these projects can adorn your mantelpiece or display cabinet. A combination of text, illustrations, and photographs accompanies each project. Once your keepsakes are displayed in an album, it becomes much easier to enjoy and share your special moments with others, and gives an added dimension to your reminiscences.

Despite the boom of computer technology, books have not lost their appeal. They have an important role to play in our lives, whether they carry the written word or take the form of a scrapbook to store data and documents. The experience of holding a well-loved album is very special and cannot be compared to holding a computer printout or looking at a screen.

Whether you want to store your album as a keepsake or include it in a display, always give yourself the chance of adding mementos. Make sure you choose the right sort of album: a ringbinder or postbound volume, for example. You will be surprised at how quickly the years roll by. Remember to relive the times of your life, using our selection of projects—or create your own, drawing from the ideas in the Inspirational sections of the book. But most of all—have fun!

LEFT: *To create a different look for your album, use velvet to cover it and decorate with a slip of lace and a dried leaf.*

THE BASICS

The great thing about making scrapbooks is that it is relatively inexpensive and you will have fun applying the basic skills explained in this section in a creative way. This section takes you through the basic equipment and materials that you will need. You will learn the importance of caring for and organizing your photographs, as well as how to arrange, crop, or manipulate images to create a fabulous effect. Once you have a theme and have selected the images you need, you can start making the scrapbook and then move on to embellishing it with the many creative ideas ranging from deckle-edging and stenciling to embossing and decoupage.

Materials and Equipment

The essentials are basic everyday items, such as pencils, rulers, craft knife, and scissors, along with paper and cardboard of various kinds, but there are also all manner of additional materials that you can use to embellish your work.

CUTTING

When you are cutting, always protect the work surface with either a self-healing mat or a pad of old newsprint, cardboard, or even an old telephone directory.

To cut cardboard, foam board, or any other thick material, use a steel ruler with a craft knife (scalpel). Photographs and papers can be cut with sharp scissors, though a mini-trimmer (a small paper cutter that gives sharp, straight edges) will be useful if you plan to do a lot of this type of work.

The basic equipment needed for the projects in this book is inexpensive and readily available.

ADHESIVES

Choose adhesives of archival quality that won't damage your pictures.

Glue sticks are acid-free and non-toxic, but the glue often dries out over a long period.

Check that photographic corners and tabs that are specially made for albums are of archival quality before you purchase them.

Craft glue (PVA) is suitable for paper and fabrics, though for many of the projects it is also possible to use two-sided carpet tape. It is very secure and is available inexpensively from hardware stores, but it does not allow for repositioning, so be sure how and where you want to stick something before allowing the surfaces to touch.

Photographic mounting spray does allow you to reposition items, but it can only be used on lightweight items.

PAPER AND CARDBOARD

There is a vast array of papers and cardboards to choose from.

To make album pages, use a medium-weight cardboard—around 6 oz (170 gm). Thinner papers can be put on top of this for decoration and special effects. Archival papers are acid-free, so they won't turn yellow or eat away at your photos.

For a natural effect, suitable for gardening themes or to display pressed flowers or other natural materials, use handmade papers. They are more expensive but look special.

To protect your photos, you can insert translucent glassine papers between the pages to keep the pictures from scratching each other.

MARKERS

Felt-tip pens come in a broad variety of types and colors. There are metallic colors suitable for writing on dark-colored paper. Calligraphic nibs are fun to try and can make your handwriting look beautifully elegant.

Be sure of what you are going to write before you begin—once you've made a mark with a felt-tip pen, you can't remove it. Remember that you should never use felt-tip markers on the backs of photos, because the colors can bleed through. Use a soft lead pencil instead.

Pigma Pens are useful for writing on an archival quality board, since they take on the characteristics of the paper, and the ink is waterproof and will not fade.

SEWING MATERIALS

You can use all sorts of tapes, threads, cords, and ribbons for sewing. Sewing supports depend on your design and what the book is going to be used for. The best thread for strength is bookbinder's linen thread, which is made from flax fiber and comes in various thicknesses. It is usually cream in color, being unbleached, but you can also buy it in black. If your sewing is going to show and you want a splash of color, use button thread and apply some beeswax. For case bindings, the best supports to use are linen or cotton fabric tape, which is sold by the roll. Linen tape is unbleached and made from woven flax fiber, while cotton tape is usually bleached. Where the sewing supports are going to show or be part of the design, you can let your imagination run wild. Anything from the notions counter can be used, including leather thongs, ribbons, and rubber piping, as long as they are reasonably strong. With all materials, bear in mind what you are going to do with the book and how it is going to be used. The stronger the materials, the longer the book will last.

You can record your memories alongside your photographs with a range of felt-tip pens, but use only soft lead pencils to mark the back of photos.

FOUND MATERIALS

There are any number of found or easily acquired materials that can be used to enhance your books and boxes. They are often found around the house, in junk and hardware stores, and when you are out and about. Curiously twisted driftwood can be used alongside raffia and garden twine as fastenings for journals and albums, and a treasure trove of beads for sewing and finishing can be discovered at local thrift shops and secondhand stores. Leaves, wire mesh, carved erasers, and combs can be inked and used to print decorative papers, and scraps of treasured handmade paper can be collaged or sewn together for use as an alternative covering material. Copper and brass wire can be used to decorate clasps, and little pieces of doweling or wooden skewers make wonderful toggles when carved, or painted and polished. Explore the projects in this book and look at the found materials that have been used.

Planning your Scrapbook

Although we try to keep all our photographs in one general family album, as our children grow, so do the albums, bulging with a medley of pictorial records. Now is time to take stock and start putting together a scrapbook to hold all those memories.

Perhaps now is the time to take stock, edit, and select all those old photographs and pieces of memorabilia that you have hoarded over the years. You can reorganize your collection to create albums that cover easily identifiable periods and themes, construct a baby's keepsake box that not only stores photos but holds all those other things you cherish, such as locks of hair or first socks, or compile a scrapbook specifically dedicated to your child's school years. These are personal items that you can make for your own family or give as a special present to friends.

If you decide to make a box instead of a book, within this box you can keep those cherished memorabilia that surround the birth of a baby. It becomes a place that unites souvenirs, such as your congratulations cards, your pregnancy and birth records, and photos of your newborn.

In the first part of this book we describe and illustrate the different materials and equipment you may need to complete the projects that follow. Many of these items are common household objects, which are easy to use even at your kitchen table. Once you've started embellishing, and making your own albums, you will discover exactly how simple and rewarding it can be to produce attractive and innovative presents and keepsakes.

It is important to choose papers and card stock with care. Think about how you will be using your book—for writing, painting, or simply as a scrapbook. If you are going to include objects, the paper needs to be strong enough to be up to

the job. A photo album needs thin card stock or thick handmade paper to support the photos. If you are thinking of painting the paper, then you will need special paper which won't buckle or distort.

You will need to choose embellishments that will enhance your book's purpose and add a personal touch. For a lover's album, for example, use warm and sumptuous materials—ribbon, sequins, and beads—all of which add luxury. Lace adds a lighter, more delicate feel. Objects that you have found on your travels—like sea-washed glass or leaves—can also be included in your design.

When deciding on bindings and fastenings, think about how you will be using your book. If it is often, make sure that the binding is sturdy. If you wish to add or remove pages, plan to use a binding that allows for this. If you're including mementos, make sure you have a flexible binding, and choose hard covers for a drawing journal.

When it comes to designing the covers, you can use whatever comes to hand to embellish a plain album or folder. All you need here is a little imagination and some of the basic materials suggested in the first section of this book.

BELOW: *Interesting handmade paper has been cut and torn, and mounted onto the cover of this scrapbook. The bamboo leaves embedded into the paper give an almost Oriental feel.*

Decorative Devices

With a little thought, simple techniques can be utilized to embellish your scrapbook. You don't need to be an artist to turn your books into works of art, just take some tips from this section and add the finishing touches.

DECKLE-EDGING

Special scissors—innovative and inexpensive—can be used to create a decorative edge to the pages of an album. The scissors come in a variety of patterns, from zigzags to waves and scallops, and can be used to achieve both positive and negative images. There are even versions for making decorative corners. If you prefer you can deckle-edge the photograph itself. Experiment on a photocopy first to see if the image adapts itself to deckling.

Both these photographs have been enhanced by using deckle scissors that give an attractive feathery, ragged edge to a handmade sheet of paper.

You can turn plain paper into exciting and interesting pages just by employing deckle-edge scissors. Deckle-edge scissors have a variety of attractive cutting edges and this a simple way to add interest to your scrapbook. When first using the scissors, be careful to keep the pattern consistent. Your finished work will look best if the corners are symmetrical—you can even buy special corner scissors and punches for this.

STENCILS AND TEMPLATES

You can use stencils or templates to make decorative borders, frames, and lettering. There is a wide choice of ready-made designs, or you can make your own by cutting a pattern from stencil board or template plastic.

When you use a stencil, secure it firmly in position with removable tape while you apply the color with paints, colored pens, or pencils.

STICKERS

Stickers are fun and especially easy for children to use. Most stickers come with a set of self-adhesive backing, but make sure you know where you want to put them before you peel them off since they are hard to remove once they have been applied.

DECORATIVE PUNCHES

Special punches allow you to press a shape out of cardboard or paper. Two types are available—a hand-held version has a scissor-like action, while the other has a press button. There is a wide variety of motifs and shapes, from hearts and stars to cats, houses, and cherubs. Some are designed to decorate borders and edges; others have longer handles that can make shapes in the middle of a page. Remember that the punched-out shapes are a positive image that can be used to decorate other pages.

Stickers are especially popular with children, and are the perfect materials for them to use when decorating their first scrapbook.

Decorative punches are versatile tools, working on both cardboard and paper. They also offer two decorative techniques, because the punched-out images can be utilized also.

RUBBER STAMPING

Rubber stamps in all sizes and shapes have become very popular in the past few years for decorating all manner of items. The color can be applied by pressing the stamp onto an inkpad and imprinting the image on the desired area. If you want to make a multi-colored design, color different areas of the stamp using a selection of felt-tip pens.

Stamp pads are available in many colors, including metallic finished such as silver, copper, and gold.

EMBOSSING

Embossing is similar to rubber stamping, but it is a little harder to perfect and requires some practice before you attempt it on an album. The stamps are the same, but you use an embossing pad treated with a glue-like substance that is tinted so you can see the design once you have transferred it. Onto this image you sprinkle embossing powders, available in a selection of colors including metallic gold, silver, and copper; then shake off the excess, which can be retained for reuse. Place the image under a heat source, as directed on the package, until the powder melts to create a raised (embossed) effect. Watch the process continuously to ensure that the paper, cardboard, or fabric does not burn. When it is cool, you can color the image with felt-tip pens or paint.

Once perfected, the art of embossing can provide beautiful frames for your photographs. It is especially suitable for black-and-white images.

DECOUPAGE

You can use old greeting cards, wrapping paper, magazines, and so on, to add texture and interest and to make a scrapbook special without it costing too much money. You may already have pretty cards that you have saved. Look for embossed cards with borders that can be cut out and used to frame pictures. Clip images that pick up the theme of your book from wrapper paper or old magazines.

Paper doilies and Victorian scraps can bring a feeling of tenderness and romance to a scrapbook. The lacy texture of a doily can be used to frame wedding photos, while the floral borders and sweet images of Victorian scraps are perfect for baby books.

Pressed flowers look charming surrounding a suitable photograph, as shown here. Lightly stick them with a glue stick and protect them with a sheet of glassine or acetate paper.

You can obtain books of Victorian scraps and other decoupage images from craft suppliers, making it easier to find just the right effect. Look out also for copyright-free image books, and hold on to pretty Christmas and birthday cards.

PRESSED FLOWERS

Pressed flowers provide an evocative link to many memories. Try to pick flowers when they are dry, and *never* pick rare or protected wild flowers, or those in public spaces or on private land. Select blossoms that are in good condition, since any bruising or flaws will look worse after pressing.

It is possible to press bulky flowers such as roses or peonies, but they tend to look rather squashed and not very attractive. Choose fine blossoms such as violets, primroses, and forget-me-nots, or take many-petalled flowers like dahlias apart and reassemble the dried petals into a simplified bloom in your scrapbook.

Flower presses can be purchased, or you can improvise with old newsprint, blotting paper, and bricks. Fold three large sheets of newsprint into quarters and place a piece of blotting paper in the fold. Lay the chosen flowers on the blotting paper, making sure they don't touch each other, and cover them with another piece of blotting paper. Close the newsprint and place a thin wooden board on top to even out the pressure. Put two or more bricks on the board to add weight and leave everything undisturbed for at least ten days. Choose a warm, dry place if possible—the quicker the blooms dry, the better their color will preserve.

Making Your Own Paper

Customize your scrapbooks with handmade paper using materials collected from your own garden or on any country walk. It is easy to create papers with fresh and pressed flowers, petals, seeds, grasses and leaves. Making paper can be a messy business, so keep your work space as tidy as possible and cover any surfaces with water absorbers, such as newsprint or old towels.

YOU WILL NEED

Newsprint—*to protect work surfaces and help dry sheets*

Waste paper—*you can recycle most papers, but not newsprint*

Water

Sponge

Blender or liquidizer—*this must include a circuit breaker*

Vat—*bigger than your largest mold*

Felts—*buy man-made felts or use striped viscose dishcloths (these should be twice as long as the mold and a little wider)*

Mold—*stretch plain screen mesh over a rectangular frame*

Sieve

Dried seeds, grasses, flowers, and leaves

Tweezers

Capillary matting—*available from garden centers*

Press—*a pair of melamine-faced plywood boards and four G-clamps*

Iron

Palette knife *(optional)*

Clothes line or folding clothes rack and pegs *(optional)*

Brown paper *(optional)*

PREPARED RECYCLED PULP

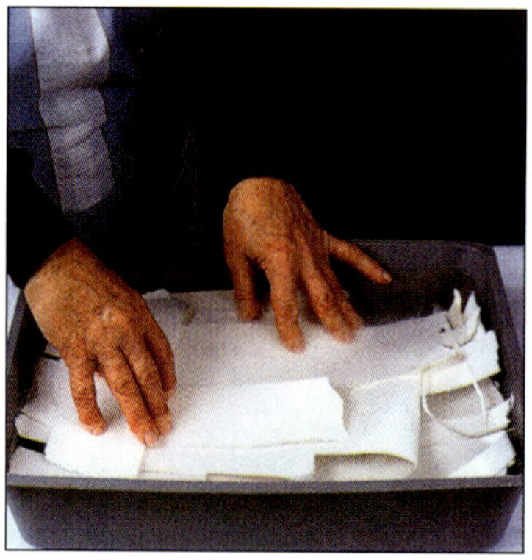

1 Soak 18 sheets of 8½ x 11 in. (22 x 28 cm) (A4) wastepaper—not newsprint—in 1 gallon (4½ liters) of water in a vat overnight.

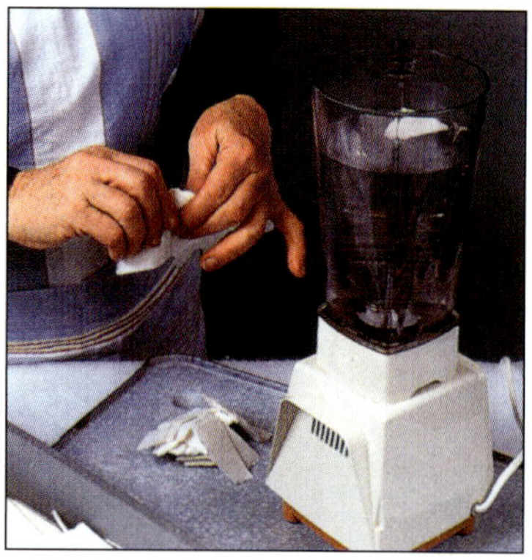

2 Tear the paper into small pieces. Fill a 1 quart (1.2 liter) kitchen blender ¾ full and add batches of paper (about 1/6 at a time). Blend to a smooth pulp.

3 Pour the pulp into a vat and repeat the process until the vat is ¾ full. Add water if necessary.

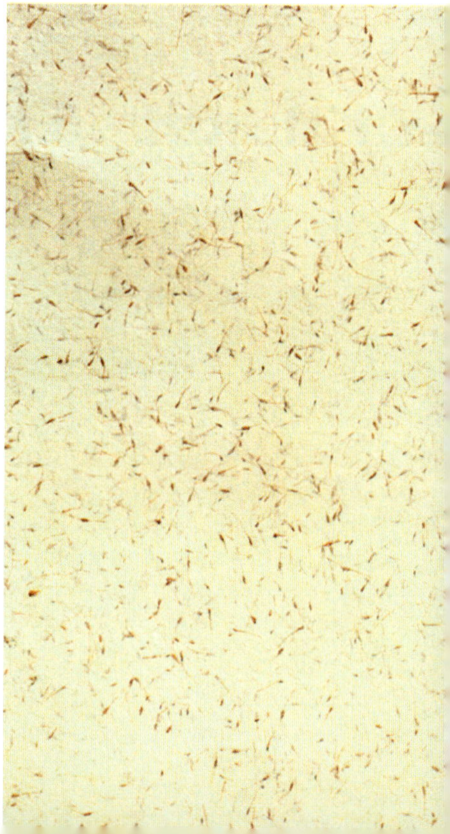

RIGHT: *Paper made from bulrush* (Cyperus papyrus). *The first paper made from papyrus appears to have been made in about 2500 to 2200 BC.*

SHEET FORMING

1 Dampen 13 felts. Fold one into a small couching pad. Place the pad under one half of another felt.

2 Stir the pulp thoroughly and let the waves subside.

3 Lower the mold vertically into the vat on the side farthest away from you. Tilt the top end downward. Pull it toward you until it is horizontal below the surface of the pulp.

4 Hold the mold horizontally and raise it out of the vat. Water will drain back into the vat.

5 If there is any unevenness on the sheet, turn the mold over and let the pulp drop back into the vat. Stir and scoop again until you have an even covering of pulp.

BULRUSH

Ideal for endpapers, this smooth textured paper is made from bulrush (also known as brown busbies, reed mace, or cattail), which commonly grows wild in ditches and at the edges of ponds and lakes. Bulrushes can be grown at home, but be careful they don't dominate your other plants.

1 Harvest the seeds by putting the rusty-brown flower spikes into a brown paper bag. Break apart the spikes in the bag, releasing the seeds. Store them in a dry place.

2 Add the seeds to prepared paper pulp and mix lightly to distribute them.

3 Form sheets and couch them as usual. Press and hang the sheets to dry.

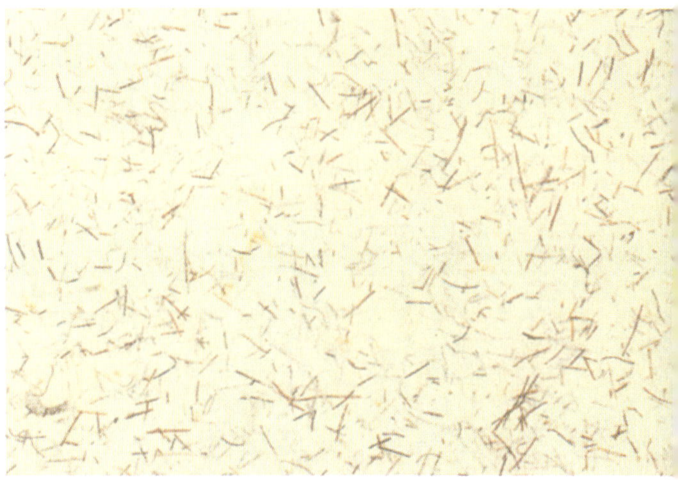

CORN ON THE COB

Paper made with silk from maize or a corn cob (*above*) has a fine texture, which makes it good to write on. Once you've removed the silks from the maize or corn, cook the cobs for a delicious snack.

1 Take the silks from the cob when it is mature. Dry in an airy place and store in a dry bag.

2 Cut the silks into small pieces and blend lightly into the prepared pulp.

3 Form sheets and couch them as usual. Press and hang the sheets to dry.

POT POURRI

Depending on the flowers and leaves you use, pot pourri can give your paper an individual tint. Lavender and rose petals work especially well.

1 Grind up seeds or spices in a coffee grinder. Crush the pot pourri to make the pieces smaller.

2 Add the seeds to prepared paper pulp and mix lightly to distribute them.

3 Form sheets and couch them as usual. Press and hang the sheets to dry.

MARIGOLD

Marigold petals come up beautifully in handmade paper, retaining their vibrant yellow color.

1 Collect marigold flower heads and remove the petals. Press the best petals between sheets of absorbent paper to dry. Dry the remaining petals.

2 Stir the unpressed petals onto the prepared pulp.

3 Form a sheet and couch it. Position the pressed petals onto the sheet with tweezers. Press, then hang the sheet to dry.

COUCHING

1 Hold the mold over the vat to drain. Position the mold over the couching pad. Turn the mold over onto the couching pad and press down.

2 Press a damp sponge onto the net to remove water. To loosen the sheet before lifting up the mold, rock the mold from side to side. Fold the other half of the felt over the sheet. Lay a fresh felt on top and start to couch your second sheet.

STORING PULP

3 Sieve the excess pulp and leave it to dry. Keep in an airtight container in a refrigerator for not longer than a week (longer in a freezer).

EMBOSSING

To make a patterned imprint on a sheet of paper, use anything with a raised pattern, for example, a leaf.

1 Form a sheet of paper and couch it.

2 Place a strongly patterned leaf on the surface of the sheet. Fold over the felt, press and dry the sheet between some newsprint.

3 When the sheet is dry, lift off the leaf with tweezers.

Experimenting With Folds

The best way to become familiar with our materials is by handling them, so try a few experimental folds of your own by doodling with some inexpensive paper.

The following diagrams and illustrations show variations on the basic accordion fold. Using papers of different weights, try folding them, and see how they behave. The thin, more fragile folds of the flutter book have a different quality to the slotted zigzag made of thin cardboard. What happens if you fold the paper at an angle, or slit one of the creases and fold in another direction? Different types of folding can be used to illustrate a poem or short story, or to create a complex maze.

A

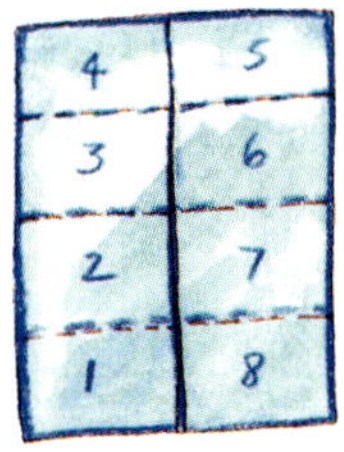

ALTERNATIVE FOLDS

Fold a flat piece of paper in half lengthwise, then fold widthwise into quarters. Open out the paper and make a slit down the middle, leaving the top fold intact (A). Fold the paper as a zigzag, start at number one and ending at number eight.

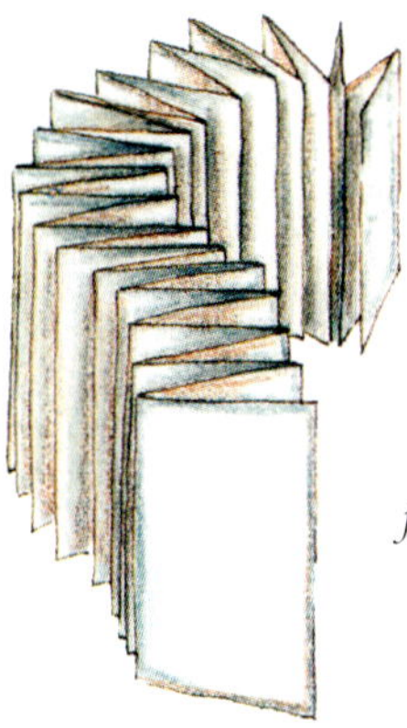

FLUTTER BOOK

Using a very thin paper such as onion skin Japanese, or bank paper, fold an extra-long zigzag. Join the folds as required and attach to a three-part board structure (as described in the foldout book section).

If you fold the zigzags unevenly, you can sculpt any number of structures. You may need to shape the lower edge (B) if you want it to stand up.

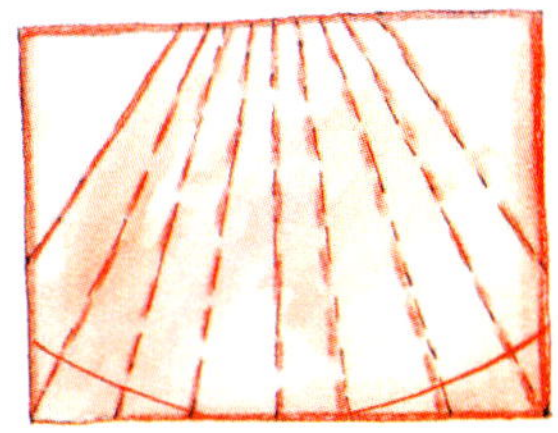

B

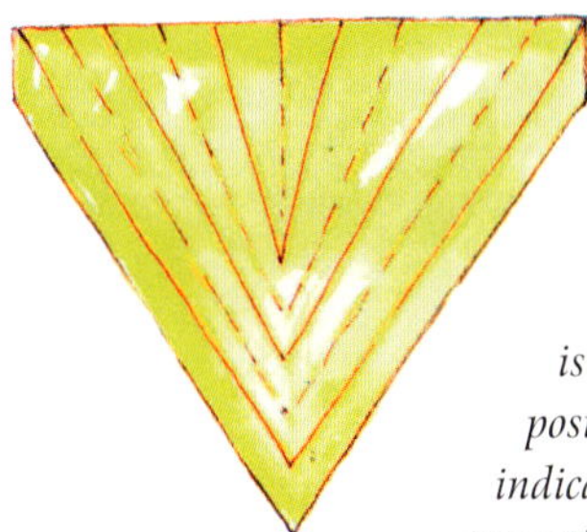

C

This fold is more complex (C) and the creases need to be measured and scored with a bone folder. Each crease line is folded both ways and then a little patience is needed to coax the folds into position. The solid and broken lines indicated show folds and reverse folds respectively.

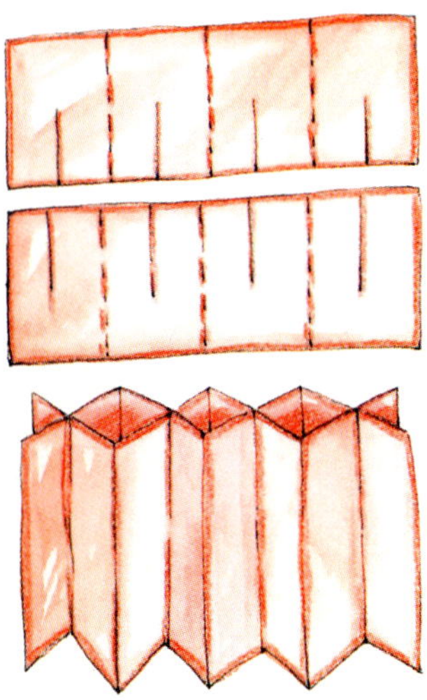

SOLID ZIGZAG BOOK

Take two pieces of stiff paper or thin cardboard cut to the same size. Score with a bone folder along the broken lines (see diagram) and make cuts half the height of the paper in the center of each fold. Fold as a zigzag, turn one upside down and slot together.

Making Your Scrapbook

There are many different ways of making a scrapbook, as the examples in this book will show you. Read these general instructions before embarking on any particular project.

EASY OPTIONS

You don't need to be artistic or adept at crafts to make a personalized scrapbook. It can be adapted from an existing album, book, or even ring-bound notebook. Decorate it to make it your own by using any of the techniques explained in Decorative Devices (see pages 14–17), ranging from the instant effect of stamps or stickers to inexpensive greeting cards. They all offer easy methods of enhancing your album without too much time or effort.

THE COVER

Covers are usually best constructed from foam board, that is light, stiff, and does not warp. It consists of a layer of styrofoam sandwiched between two pieces of cardboard. Because of its three-tier construction, you can form a hinge by cutting through the top two layers while keeping the third layer intact. Then simply bend the board so that the cut line opens up—in this way, the base layer becomes the hinge, that can be reinforced with masking or bookbinder's tape. Always use a sharp craft knift or scalpel—a blunt one will make a ragged edge—and cut against a steel ruler.

If you want the cover to bend more than 90°, make two parallel cuts ⅛–¼ in. (3–5 mm) apart and remove the two layers between them to create a gully.

COVERING FOAM BOARD

To cover foam board with paper or fabric, it is essential to make the covering material fit into the hinge. If you simply stick a piece of paper over the cut lines, you will reseal the cut and no movement will be possible. You could slit the paper along the cut to redeem the mistake somewhat, but the raw edges will show when the cover is bent, so always study the steps before you begin a project.

BINDING THE PAGES

Most of the pages need to be made from heavy paper or lightweight cardboard. They can be any color that is appropriate to the theme of your scrapbook. Of course, the number of pages you make will affect the structure of the book—the more pages there are, the stronger the book must be. In our projects we show several methods of construction, ranging from spiral binding to stitching to ring binders. Holes can be made with a paper or leather punch and the pages held together with metal posts or tied with cord or ribbon. You can copy traditional scrapbooks or albums that have a margin folded over the spine edge of each page to allow for the thickness of photographs, and you can insert a sheet of protective glassine paper between the pages.

PUTTING IN BULKY AND LOOSE ITEMS

Sometimes you may want to include non-paper items in your book, or you may wish to leave things loose for easy removal.

For a small, delicate item such as a shell, you can cut a window through one or more pages to the depth of the item, and these protective surrounding pages can be glued together or left loose. Hobby and collector's suppliers sell many types of plastic pockets and pouches designed for displaying items such as coins and stamps. Some have a self-adhesive backing that can be stuck into a scrapbook; others need to be glued in place.

Files of the type used to store photographic slides can be useful for an assortment of loose items; and envelopes, both large and small, can be glued or taped into a book to hold letters, certificates, and the like. You may need to remove the facing page to reduce bulkiness in the book.

To make a cover take a piece of foam board and mark two parallel lines for the spine. Using a metal ruler and a craft knife cut through the top two layers of the board, leaving the third layer intact.

Next, bend the foam board slightly so that the cut lines open and remove the top two layers.

Finally, when covering the foam board make sure the decorative paper fits into the hinge to enable movement.

Managing your Photographs

Don't leave your photos to curl up in a shoebox. Catalog them and put them into albums where they will be protected, and it will be much easier to share your pleasure in them. Here are some tips to help you.

SELECTION

It is always hard to choose what to put into an album from the boxes of photographs that we have. The task can be made easier if you limit your albums or scrapbooks to particular subjects or specific dates, as we have done in this book. Once you have decided on the theme of your book, you can sort and edit the appropriate pictures. Try to clear a large clean work surface to spread them out on. Make sure your hands are clean; to prevent fingerprints, wear cotton gloves.

Choose those photos that best capture the time and feeling of your subject. If you have several similar pictures, select the one with the best exposure, the most clarity, or the best expressions.

CROPPING

Cropping really starts with the eye before you take the picture. Decide what you want in the photo and check that it fits the frame without too much superfluous information. Make sure you don't cut off a person's feet or the top of a building, unless this is the desired effect. We all end up with some pictures that are badly framed or have boring or distracting backgrounds, but by cropping, we can improve the final image.

To experiment with suitable crops, make two L-shaped corners from cardboard and put them together over the photo to create a movable "frame." Adjust its size until you find a crop that you like. Make a light pencil mark where the photo is to be cropped and cut along the line with scissors, a craft knife and ruler, or a mini-trimmer. If you want to cut your pictures into shapes, such as hearts, ovals, or hexagons, use a ready-made stencil, or cut your own from cardboard. Draw around a cookie cutter or other shape, if you wish. Check that the shape fits the photo and suits the subject matter visually.

PHOTOGRAPHING A SCENE

It is difficult to give the impression of an entire environment in a single shot. Try standing in the same place, marked with chalk or tape, and move the camera to take slightly overlapping shots that can be pieced together. The seams are less obvious if you cut around shapes that overlap.

PHOTOGRAPHING A SEQUENCE

A sequence of pictures can be taken in quick succession to capture an event or a mood, and then mounted together to add movement and liveliness.

PHOTOMONTAGE

You can create a big picture from lots of smaller ones put together. Scale doesn't matter as long as you can make the pieces work together visually. Choose the photos that you want to use for the background first, and build the picture up from there. If a white edge shows up noticeably along a cut, shaped edge, use a felt-tip pen to color the background to blend it in. Once you have created a pleasing arrangement, make a

Cropping starts with your eye; decide what information you want in a picture and edit out any superfluous details with your camera. If this isn't possible, you can always crop your photograph.

chart of it, so that you know where each piece belongs when you remove the photos to apply adhesive to them. Spray photographic mounting adhesive on the backs of the photos and lay the image on the mounting sheet, starting with the background.

PHOTOCOPYING

This is a cheap and effective way to reproduce pictures, especially if you have lost your negatives. It also allows you to enlarge or reduce photos easily. Photocopying techniques are developing and improving all the time, as well as becoming cheaper. The main differences between the original photo and most copies are the thickness of the paper and the matt surface, although there is a photographic-type paper that gives a glossy finish.

If you want to reproduce several photographs at a time, it is most economical to stick the originals on a sheet of paper before copying. If you want to copy old sepia photographs, use a color copier, not a standard black-and-white one.

PHOTO TRANSFERS

Print and photocopy stores can copy photographs onto transfer paper which can be put into a heat press that will transfer the image onto fabric. Clean, white 100 percent cotton material is best.

LAMINATING

Photographs or photocopies can be layered between two sheets of clear plastic and heat-sealed, or laminated, for strength and durability. Before you create your image, ask the copy store for advice about thicknesses, since using more than one layer can sometimes cause the plastic to bubble.

Personalize your scrapbook with a favorite photograph or picture. Your local photocopy or print store can transfer it for you. Stitch the cloth onto the front as decoration. Choose thread and fabric ties to complement your picture.

Making a Photo Grid

A perfect way of storing your holiday photographs and postcards is by making a grid, and it is easy to add in or take out more whenever you wish.

1 Stick a square of fabric onto the page with glue.

2 Criss-cross strips of silver thread or elastic diagonally across the material about 2 in. (5 cm) apart.

3 Secure with copper sticky tape around the edge of the material and insert your photos and postcards.

Photomontage

If you enjoy photography and acquire hordes of photographs that never find their way into albums, why not use them to experiment with photomontage, to create new and exciting pages in your scrapbook.

Photomontage involves the manipulation of the photographic image and is as old a practice as photography itself. The history of the art form dates from direct-contact printing of real items such as leaves and flowers, through to double exposures, and finally to cutting out and reassembling photographs. Of course it is not necessary to always use your own photographs, and the invention of the photocopier allows infinite manipulation of the image you would like to use. The basis of the photomontaged image depends on the quality of the original pictures and how they are used.

PHOTOCOPY MANIPULATION

By using a photocopier (either color or black-and-white), you can enlarge, reduce, zoom in on, flip, stretch, and even compress an image. Images can be turned from positive into negative, and have their tone and color altered to suit the color of your background pages. Someone who is experienced in using photocopiers can instruct you on how to achieve the best results. Plan your image (possibly using a rough first) and organize the things you will need before you manipulate the component parts on a copier, so that you do not waste time and money on copies that you are unable to use; for example, if you have made them the wrong size.

Once you have decided the nature of the imagery, you can start to manipulate it and cut it up accordingly. Before you begin, decide on the dimensions of the finished piece and where the main focus will be. Is it all foreground detail, or is there a depth of field and sense of perspective? You can then manipulate and juxtapose your pictures accordingly to give the best effect.

Archiving your Photographs

In years gone by, black-and-white photographs were used to record family events. Now we can utilize technical developments to preserve our treasured memories.

If you plan to store your photographs in a bookshelf album, choose one with a sturdy cover that will withstand frequent handling. Using ring binders gives you the advantage of being able to add or reorganize your photos, although they may not be as attractive as display albums, that are normally bound with leather or linen. Scrapbooks are a good way of storing your photographs and you can try various ways of displaying your pictures until they are esthetically pleasing. Another way of storing your photos is in a post-bound album, that contains punched pages held together by metal posts.

Unless photos are stored correctly, damage and deterioration will result. Magnetic page albums tend to cause photos to fade and discolor, and plastic overlays can turn the paper pages yellow or brown. It is sometimes difficult to remove photos that have been glued in; rubber cement (rubber-based contact adhesive), in

This page from a family scrapbook was compiled by a cat lover. The photographs and drawings have been held together visually with rubber stamps and glued-on sequins. It is a fun project to do with your children.

particular, causes discoloration, so archival glue should be used. Reactions between the plastic film and photos in pocket-page albums are also common, as the plastic eats away at the pictures. Avoid this problem with pockets made from polyester, polyethylene, polypropylene, or triacetate. Scrapbooks with construction-paper pages have a high acid content, and you may find that the paper itself fades before the pictures do, so look for scrapbooks with low-acid pages.

Storage conditions also play an important role when preserving photographs. You are probably aware that storing your photographs in direct sunlight causes oxidation that sets off chemical changes, while humidity and moisture both facilitate fungal growth. But perhaps you didn't know that cardboard boxes and shoeboxes release harmful gases that may tarnish pictures over time, so must be avoided. The low-grade fiber and additives that make up brown envelopes will have the same effect. Also, take care to keep dirt and dust away from your photographs to prevent their surfaces from being scratched.

You should store photographs in rooms you live in, rather than in attics or basements, ideally in temperatures between 65 and 70°F (18 and 21°C).

You will find that photographs, once stored and archived correctly, can last for many years. Remember, though, that photography is a chemical process and photographs are subject to ongoing deterioration. Good-quality materials, conditions, and storage are vital to longevity. Acid-free and lignin papers are excellent preservers used by many archivists, together with high-quality plastic film and other durable materials. Black-and-white pages are ideal for display, and parchment dividers will protect pictures from dust and chemical reactions.

When writing on photographs, limit yourself to a soft lead pencil, since felt-tip pens can bleed through and the marks made by a ballpoint pen may also show. Always index and label your photos with dates, themes, and comments. Label negatives separately in acid-free envelopes, and store them in heavy-duty shoebox-sized boxes especially made for storing photographs, packed tightly so they cannot curl.

Since color photographs fade more quickly than monochrome ones, you might want to document important events, such as the arrival of a new pet, moving to a new house, a special trip, or a party, using black-and-white film to provide a memory bank that will last for generations to come.

Be sure of what you are going to write in your book before you begin—once you've made a mark with a felt-tip pen, you can't remove it. Remember that you should never use felt-tip markers on the backs of photographs because the colors can bleed through to the other side.

COVER DESIGN

You can use whatever comes to hand to embellish a plain scrapbook or folder. All you need is a little imagination and some of the basic materials suggested at the beginning of this book. By adding texture to the papers you use, your covers can become more sophisticated and eye-catching. Plain paper that has been hand-painted and stenciled adds an individual touch to your album. The following few pages give you the information you need to create some lovely ideas for your cover. Clear, practical suggestions on techniques help you explore a variety of creative possibilities and offer expert tips as you experiment with color, texture, and composition.

PAINTED TEXTURES

Using paint to create your own "surface" on store-bought papers requires only a few simple tools and is easily done. Preparing your own papers will add a personal touch to your covers, and allows a greater choice of colors, textures, and surface finishes.

Any type of paint may be used including watercolor, oil, acrylic, gouache, or poster paint. Acrylic will give a flat surface, whereas watercolor can be used for a very subtle and watery paint surface. Oil paint can be applied in a thicker consistency for a textured effect. Gouache can be used in the same way as watercolor, but allows for a richer, more opaque color if required.

The method you use to apply paint to paper will alter the overall effect of your work. Applying the color with different-sized paint brushes will add interest to the paper and give a variety of brush marks. Try a wide decorator's brush or an old toothbrush, as well as standard painting brushes. In addition to basic brushes, a great many household objects can be used to apply color to paper. Try using old rags, combs, and even your fingers.

Vary the strength of the paint and amount of water used when mixing the paint. Thick paint with a small amount of water will give a dark and textured effect, whereas thinner paint using lots of water will create a pale and watery effect.

Graduated paint effects Graduated paint effects can be achieved by increasing the amount of water used as you paint a sheet of paper. Start with thick watercolor paint (a little water and lots of pigment) and as you fill the page, add more water to the mixed paint. This will make the last area painted very watery and much paler than the first section painted. This effect can also be used to graduate from one color to another. Mix two colors—for example, orange, and red. Begin by painting the orange. When you have painted half the paper, add some red paint and merge the two colors together using water. Continue by painting pure red at the bottom of the paper.

Have a jar of clean water at hand when mixing paint colors. Change the water regularly to keep the colors clean.

Brush marks How much water you use when painting these brush marks will also alter their effect. Using very little water will encourage definite brush marks; adding lots of water evens out the brush marks and creates a watery effect. The technique here is an exercise to show how to make definite brush marks and how to eliminate them.

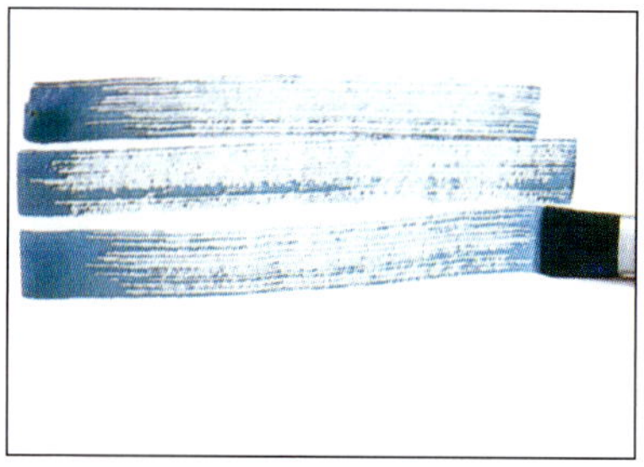

1 Using a creamy consistency of paint, paint bold strokes from side to side across a sheet of paper. The brush should be damp enough to carry paint across the page and leave definite marks.

2 Add a little water to the paint and wet the brush thoroughly. Starting at the top of the page, sweep the brush over the paint several times. The now-watery paint should eliminate the dry brush-marked areas.

3 The paint can be left with areas of brush marks, or it can all be painted over to produce a softer, more watery effect.

LEFT: *A variety of other textured paint effects can be achieved by painting with your fingers, using a foam roller dipped in paint, or swirling a paint-covered comb.*

MARBLING

In the world of paper and paper arts, marbling, or the Japanese *suminagashi*, is without doubt the most delightful and enchanting technique. It is so simple that anyone may achieve successful results.

Based on the principle that oil and water do not mix, marbling involves floating an oil-based substance in several colors on the surface of water. The colors can be manipulated into patterns or left to form random swirls. A sheet of paper is placed on the surface and carefully peeled off, revealing the pattern of colors. Many wonderful books have been covered using marbled paper, and here is a beginner's guide to get you started.

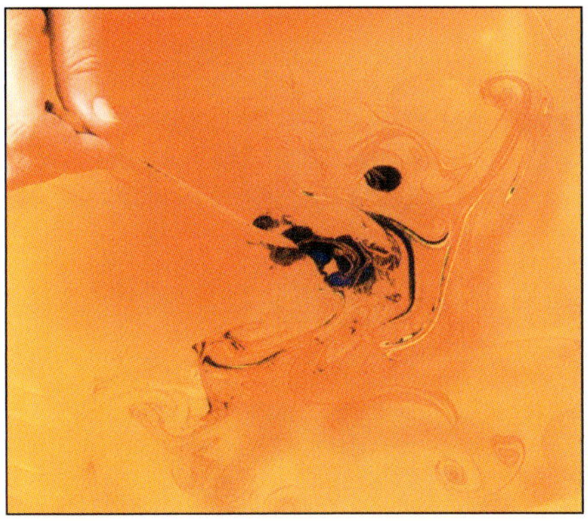

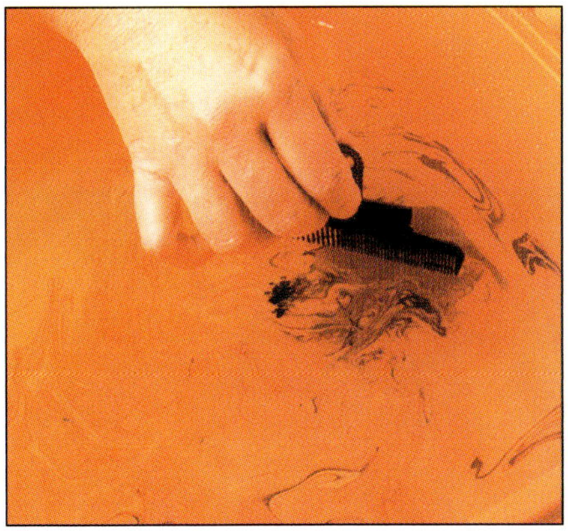

1 Fill the pan with 2–3 in. (5–7 cm) water. Apply a dot of marbling ink to the water. Some marbling kits contain a small blotting paper dot for dispersing the inks.

2 Apply a drop of each color to the first dot and watch as the colors spread across the surface. If using oil paints thinned with mineral spirits, use a toothbrush to spatter color across the water's surface.

3 Using a toothpick or sharp stick, gently pull the colors. Here a fine-tooth comb attached to a clip is used to pull the colors a little more. Avoid stirring the ink as this will blend all the colors into a rather muddy sameness.

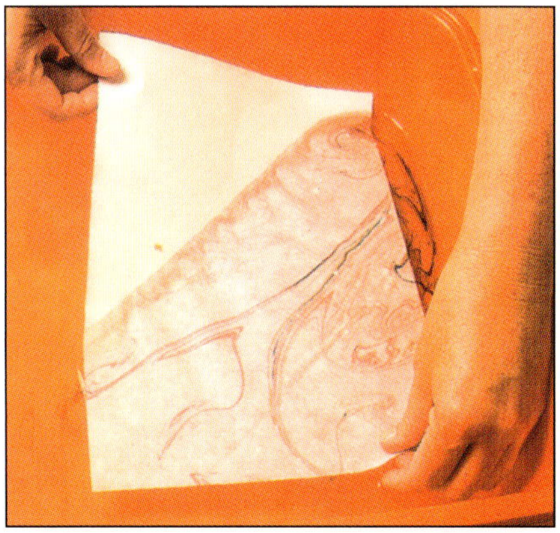

4 Gently lower the sheet of abaca paper onto the surface of the water.

5 If you hold the sheet of abaca paper at diagonally opposite corners when lowering it into the water, you will allow yourself a little more control. Allow the paper to "roll" gently onto the water.

6 Lift the sheet out of the pan by the corners in one smooth motion and place it to dry, pattern side up, on a pad of newsprint.

FOLD AND DIP

This variation on the tie-dye theme of the 1960s uses paper instead of fabric and bears some resemblance to the Japanese art of *shibori-zome* that combines intricate knot-tying with dyeing to create beautiful patterns.

This simplified version uses a sheet of abaca, that is strong enough to withstand all the handling necessary. For even greater effect use a sheet that has been scrunched and then dried.

1 Begin with a damp sheet for sharp creases and better spreading of the dye. Spray water over a dry sheet to dampen it.

2 Start to fold the sheet of damp abaca into a fan.

3 Use a bone folder to crease the edges. If a bone folder is unavailable, use a spoon handle or other strong but blunt edge that will crease but not tear the paper.

4 Make folds about ⁴⁄₅ in. (2 cm) wide. You can experiment with smaller or larger fold widths to create more intricate or interesting patterns.

5 Starting at one end of the folded fan, fold the tip into a triangular shape. Crease with a bone folder.

6 Fold the triangle back, and continue to fold back and forth.

7 When all that remains is a little triangular bundle, use a clamp to hold the bundle securely, exposing a corner.

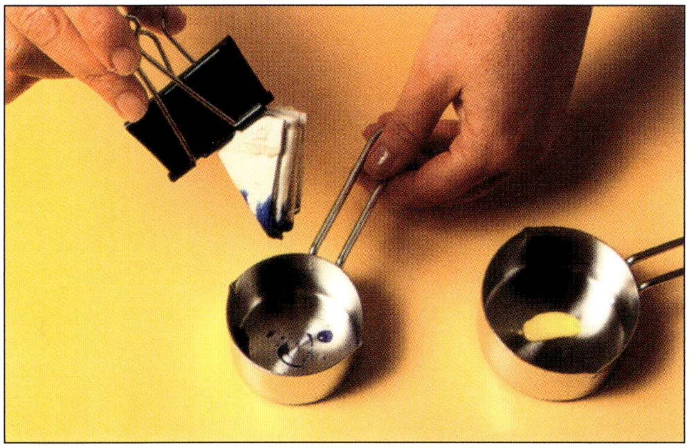

8 Dip the corner of the clamped bundle first into one color of ink, and then into a second color. Repeat with the other two corners, moving the clamp as necessary.

9 Allow to air-dry overnight. Open out the folded abaca to reveal a kaleidoscope of color and pattern.

TEXTURED FINISH USING A TOOTHBRUSH

Paint a sheet of paper with a base color. Mix a watery consistency of paint. Dip an old toothbrush in the paint and, pointing it away from you, hold the toothbrush over the painted paper. Use your forefinger to flick or splash paint marks over the colored background. You could mix another color and splash it on in the same way.

A slightly bolder effect can be achieved by firmly flicking the whole toothbrush downward while you hold it over the paper.

LEFT: *The cover of this scrapbook has been made using marbled paper (see page 35 for details).*

REPEAT PATTERN

Repeated patterns work particularly well when combined with collage. Sheets of pattern can be used as backgrounds or can be torn to leave fragmented pieces.

One of the easiest ways to create random pattern is by using a potato as a printing block.

Carefully cut a potato in half. Cut a design into the surface of the potato, making sure you have cut away all unwanted areas. Mix some paint to a fairly thick consistency and apply it to the potato using a sponge. Test the print on scrap paper. Print randomly across the page. When the print is dry, you could print a second time using another color.

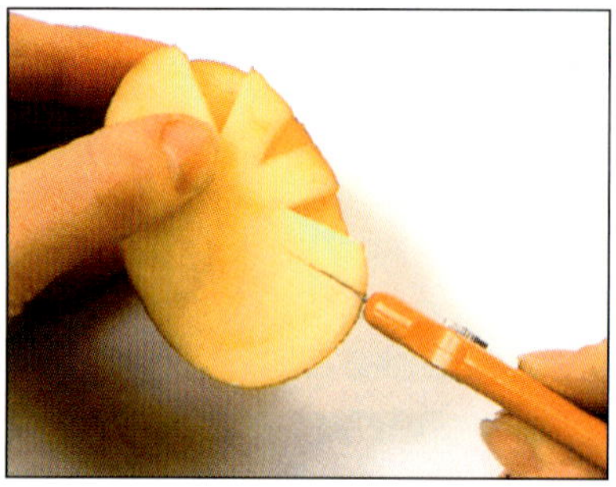

1 Carefully cut a large potato in half. Press the cut edge on paper towel to remove any excess moisture. Using a craft knife, carefully cut a simple shaped design into the cut edge of the potato. The design must have a flat surface so that it prints evenly. Cut away any excess potato from around the shape.

2 Mix some paint to a smooth, thick consistency. Use a sponge to cover the potato shape with paint. Test the potato print on scrap paper first. Press the painted potato firmly down onto the paper. Be careful not to move it around; this will smudge the image.

3 When printing the repeat pattern, keep applying fresh paint to the potato shape. You could sketch where you want to place the printed images on scrap paper before you start.

Consider the choice of paper for your background. Excellent effects can be achieved by printing onto foil, clear acetate, construction paper, or even tracing paper.

ADDING COLOR

Applying color to black-and-white surfaces is one way of lending a more personal approach to your work. Ordinary everyday images can be transformed into more personal elements ready for use on the cover of your scrapbook. Your choice of colors will reflect your own style much more than store-bought papers and materials.

The choice of colors for applying onto black-and-white images will depend on the subject matter of that image. Before using any colors, experiment until you find a combination that you think fits the image. Consider whether you would like the colored image to be realistic. An unexpected color palette can result in highly original finished work. Other mediums can be used to color black-and-white images. Try experimenting with chalk pastel on newsprint, oil pastel on photocopies, and fiber-tipped pens on photographs.

ADDING COLOR TO NEWSPRINT

1 Flatten out a sheet of newsprint. Mix paint to a medium milky consistency. Using a flat brush and broad sweeping strokes, cover the newsprint with paint.

2 Leave some areas free of paint, and completely cover other areas. Agitate the newsprint, turning it gently from side to side, to alter the effect of the paint. Blot the newsprint with paper towel to remove excess water and leave an interesting texture on the surface.

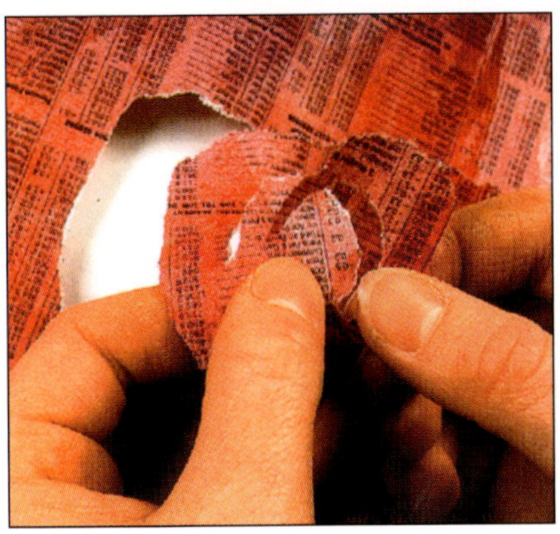

3 Rip patterns and strips from the painted newsprint. Ignore the text and images, using them purely as a textural effect.

ADDING COLOR TO PHOTOCOPIES

1 Using good-quality black-and-white photocopies of your sketch, lightly sand the surface using fine sandpaper.

2 Mix a watery consistency of paint and start to outline your sketch. Finish the paintwork by covering an area of the background to make it look as if your subject was originally drawn on a colored background.

3 On the finished image, the unpainted edges of the photocopy have been ripped away.

4 You could try painting strange colors over a whole photocopy to give the whole image a quirky effect.

Making Corners and Finishing Edges

Cover papers and cloths are cut to extend ¾ in (2 cm) beyond the edges of the board to be covered. This extension is called the "turn-in." Before the covering material is turned in, its corners must be cut. Both the angle of this cut and its distance from the tip of the board are crucial.

Apply adhesive to the covering material and press the board into position. Trim the corners at a 45° angle. The distance between the tip of the board and this cut should measure 1½ times the thickness of the board. If you cut too closely, the tip of the board is exposed. If you cut too far away, the corner is klutzy. After cutting all corners, reapply adhesive to the turn-ins if necessary.

Starting with the head and tail, bring the turn-ins onto the board. First, using your bone folder, crease the material against the board edge. Second, flatten the material onto the board, pressing out any air pockets or bubbles. Use your thumbnail to pinch in the small sharp triangles of material at the corners. Press firmly so that the material hugs the corner and molds itself around the board. With your folder, gently tap all corners, eliminating any sharp points or loose threads.

ALTERNATE CORNERS FOR FRAGILE PAPERS

When wet, fragile or thin papers tend to tear. A universal or library corner involves no cutting and is recommended. This treatment is inappropriate for heavyweight papers or cloth; the resulting corner would be too bulky. After pasting the paper and centering the board on it, fold one corner triangle onto the board. Using your bone folder, shape the paper against the board thickness on both top (head) and side (fore-edge). Firmly press the remaining bits (right side of the paper) onto the turn-ins below. Repeat at the other corners. With your finger, dab a dot of paste onto the turn-ins, near the corners. Complete the turn-ins (as in above directions). This corner covering yields a gentle, slightly rounded corner.

FOR FRAGILE PAPERS

Using Found Objects

The exciting thing about designing covers with found objects is that there is such a wide variety of material to choose from—the creative possibilities are limitless.

One of the greatest pleasures is recognizing the potential of things you see around you every day and building up a collection of material that can be used on the covers of your scrapbook. This material may be found in the countryside, the garden, the street, the beach, or the home—wherever you are there will be objects to discover and collect.

Collecting objects and recycling them can be creative in itself. It is very satisfying to know that a discarded radio or clock can be taken apart and its components used in making a new and exciting object. When friends and relatives know what you are doing, they will often share your enthusiasm and bring you envelopes or boxes of bits and pieces that they have discovered themselves.

It is a good idea to get into the habit of carrying clean bags or small boxes and tissue paper with you as often as possible so that you can keep interesting objects together and safe until you can return home and add your "treasures" to your collection.

ALTERING OBJECTS

Found items can be used as they are or altered to create new and unique shapes. For example, shells, bones, circuit boards, and brittle objects can be broken down with pliers, paper can be cut, torn, crumpled, and folded, while dried leaves and fabrics can also be cut or torn to almost any shape.

COLOR AND TONE

By using the color and tone of the objects in your collection, you can produce a wide variety of effects. Light objects show up more clearly on a dark ground and dark objects on a light ground. But for more subtle effects, experiment with using objects of a similar tone but different color, for example, red berries on a dark green surface. The harshness of metallic objects can be subdued when used with warm reds and oranges.

It is also possible to transform dull objects by painting them using acrylic paint, which dries much more quickly than oil paint. Look at the objects in your collection and try brightening some of the duller ones with bold colors.

Wire, which can be found in a wide variety of colors and thicknesses, can be twisted into many different shapes and trimmed to fit a particular space.

Making a Soft Cover

Consider the purpose and binding method of the book when choosing whether to use a soft or hard cover. Some binding methods are more suited to a soft cover, such as the buttonhole stitch. Others work well with either a soft or hard cover, such as the Japanese or stab binding method.

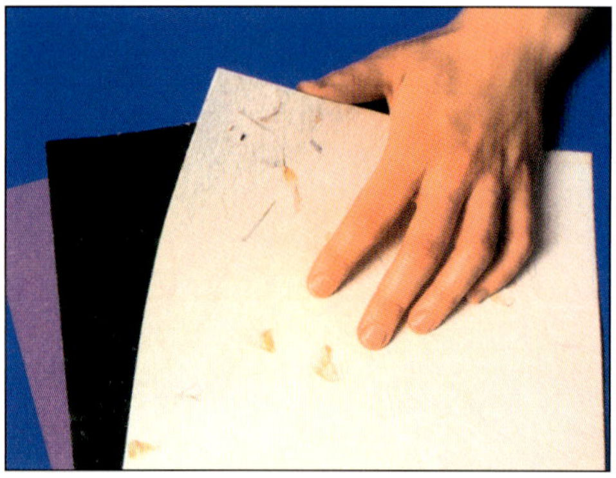

1 Choose the paper for your cover. Card-weight paper is excellent for preparing a soft-cover book. There are many options open to you, for example, textured papers from specialty paper stores, heavy handmade papers, that are made by adding extra pulp to the vat in order to pull very thick sheets, and corrugated cardboard with an exposed flute, available in a range of flute designs and colors.

2 To prepare a soft cover for your scrapbook, first measure the dimensions of the inside pages.

3 Mark the dimensions on the cover paper. Select a paper that is flexible enough to fold, but strong enough to withstand use.

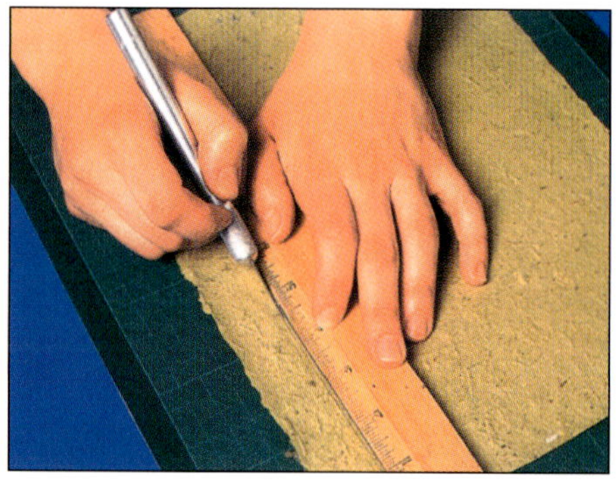

4 Using a craft knife and ruler with a metal edge, trim the paper to the marked dimensions.

5 Once trimmed, the cover paper will be folded, the pamphlet section stitched, or pasted securely. Score the line on the cover to create a crisp fold.

6 Fold along the scored line. This cover is now suitable for being sewn on to your inside pages.

Making a Hard Cover

Before making a hard cover think about the message you are trying to convey. A hard cover imparts a more formal appearance to a book than a soft cover. It protects delicate inside pages and helps to keep the book closed. Hard covers may therefore be more suited to a scrapbook that has a lot of pages.

1 Using a craft knife and metal-edged ruler, cut the heavyweight bookbinding board into three pieces: a back cover measuring 5 x 7 in. (12 x 18 cm), a front cover measuring 5 x 5½ in. (12 x 14 cm) and a front spine measuring 5 x 1 in. (12 x 2.5 cm). Using a metal-edged ruler, trim the board for the back cover. Trim the front cover and spine piece to fit the text block.

2 Place a natural abaca covering paper on the work surface, with the right side facing down. Place the back cover on the paper and draw around the edge with a pencil. This outline will give you a guide for positioning the front cover and spine pieces. Trim the excess paper leaving 1–2 in. (2.5–5 cm) around the edge of the cover marking.

3 Practice positioning the front cover and spine by first placing the front cover on the paper. Position it within the traced back cover, flush with the right-hand side. Now place the spine flush with the left-hand side. This should leave a gap between the front cover and spine of around ½ in. (1.5 cm). This gap will later become the hinge of the book.

4 Apply wheat paste to the natural abaca cover paper, spreading it from the center of the paper to the outer edges.

5 Place the front cover carefully on the pasted paper.

6 Place the spine onto the pasted paper.

7 Flip the piece over and smooth the paper with a brayer, rolling it from the center of the cover to the outer edges. Continue until the paper is free of air bubbles and creases.

8 With the coverboard-side up, apply wheat paste to the edges and corners of the paper.

9 Miter the corners by folding each corner to a 45° angle.

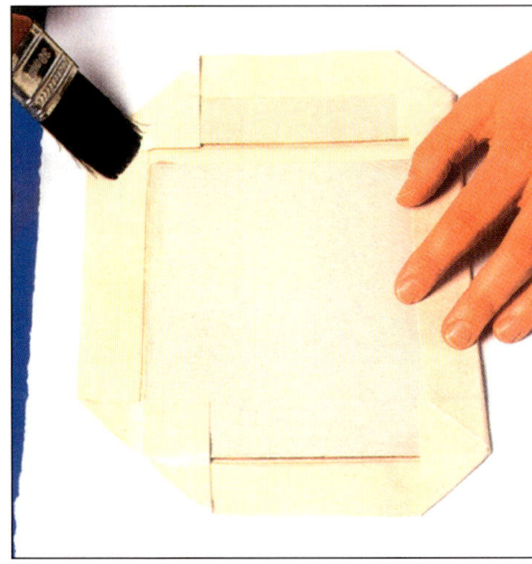

10 Apply paste to the edges of the cover paper.

11 Use a bone folder to wrap the paper tightly around the edges. Carefully pull the paper taut and smooth it onto the back of the cover.

12 Fold the spine edge toward the center and smooth the edge with a bone folder.

13 Use a moss-green abaca paper to paste onto the inside of the cover. Cut the paper to cover most of the inner cover with a ¼–½ in. (6–12 mm) margin. Brush paste onto the inside cover paper.

16 Place the wet cover between layers of waxed paper and flat board. Weigh down with bricks and leave for 24 hours.

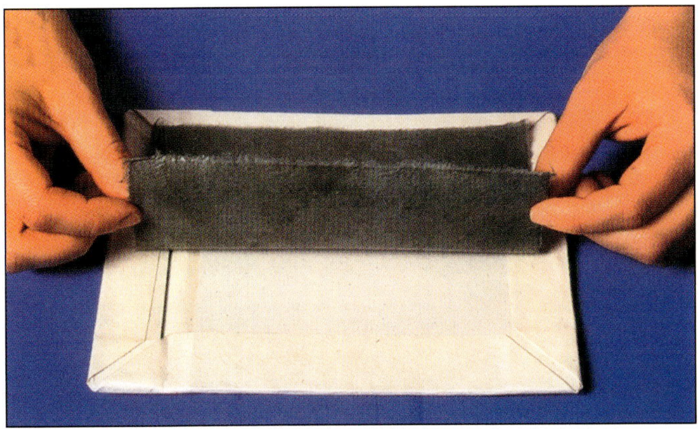

14 Position the paper on the back of the cover.

15 Use a brayer to smooth the paper, rolling from the center toward the outer edge.

You can use the hard covers to make a stylish stab-bound book such as the one shown here.

Making a Fabric Cover

This fabric-covered scrapbook is very unusual and could be a highly personal gift. For this particular cover a heart design has been used, but you can choose any design that may suit the content of your book.

1 Cut two pieces of thick cardboard 6½ in. (17 cm) square and tape them together using masking tape. Make sure they can fold easily.

2 Using handmade paper, cover the outside of this cardboard cover. Cut six lengths of double-sided sticky tape about 5 in. (12 cm) long. Attach the strips along the edges of the cardboard cover. Fold the edges over and secure them with double-sided tape.

3 Turn the corners in with a sharp crease. When you are satisfied that the cover can open and close easily, fold over the two shorter edges and press firmly onto the sticky tape.

4 Tear a sheet of watercolor paper into four or five rectangles of 6 x 12 in. (15 x 30 cm) each. If you crease the paper sharply first it should tear easily. Fold these rectangles in half to form pages. Using a strong, white thread, sew them together along the center crease with three large stitches.

5 Using lengths of double-sided tape stuck onto the outside two pages of watercolor paper, stick the pages into the book cover. Again, don't stick them firmly until you are sure the book will open and close properly.

6 Select and cut out the fabrics 4¼ x 5½ in (11 x 14 cm) to form the base of the appliquéd piece. You will need a piece of brown cotton and a slightly larger piece of cotton check with the edges pinked. Remember, the fabric must fit onto the cover of the book but leave a border of the handmade paper showing.

7 Select the fabrics for the flowers, stems, container, and other shapes. Iron paper-backed fusible bonding web onto the wrong side of each one. Using a pencil, draw the shapes on the back of the bonded fabric and cut them out.

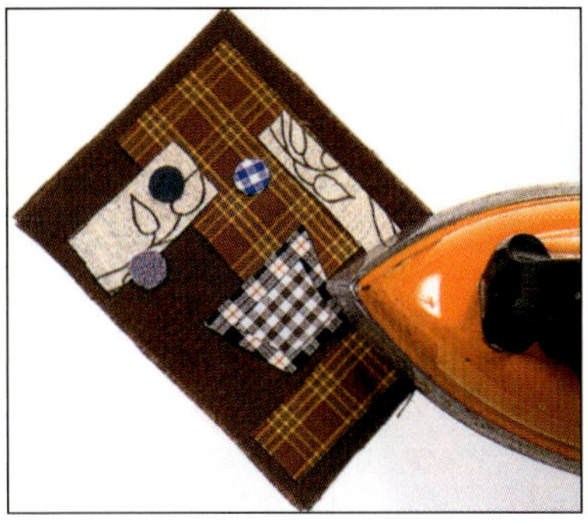

8 When all the shapes are cut out, peel off the backing paper and arrange the pieces on the brown-fabric background. Make sure the non-bonded side is facing up, and carefully press with an iron so the bonding web adheres to the background, securing the shapes in position.

9 Secure some of the shapes with small stitches along the edges of the pieces. Other shapes can be sewn with large stitches and embroidery thread. Use this thread to sew large, uneven stitches on the piece as extra features.

10 Place double-sided tape on the reverse side of the picture's edges and center. Carefully place the picture in the center of the chequered fabric background and stick down firmly. Stick double-sided tape along the edges of the checked base fabric. Hold the finished piece over the front cover of the book until it is in position; then press to secure it.

Painting and Dyeing Fabric

Although there is a wide choice of fabrics available nowadays, you will have a far more original scrapbook design if you dye and decorate your own. Not only that, it will be a lot more fun.

Some fabrics will not hold dyes, but some, such as cottons, silks, and linens, are ideal. There's no end to the different effects that you can produce, and the techniques range from the most simple and basic to the more complicated and skilled.

ADDING COLOR AND PATTERN

The fabrics being dyed or patterned do not need to start off solid (plain) white. Exciting results often come from dyeing materials that are already patterned, such as ginghams or small florals, or worked on top of a fabric that has already been dyed.

The advantage of dyeing and decorating fabrics yourself is that it allows you to get the exact colors and patterns you want, harmonizing and matching styles, and it also produces a unique result.

Whatever technique you try, use your imagination. Don't be afraid to experiment until you get the result you really want.

DYEING

Dyeing fabrics at home has never been easier. Fabric dyes are readily available in a wide choice of colors, and they are generally very simple to use. Colors can be mixed together to vary the tone, and experimentation is very much the key here.

Tie-dyeing is a very easy technique and produces wonderful results. Silk and light cottons are the easiest to tie-dye, and often work best. There are many methods of tie-dyeing; once you become more confident in the basic techniques, you can experiment and make up your own methods.

THE ART OF BATIK

Batik is an extremely useful technique, but as a proper wax pot is needed, it can prove costly. The pot melts the wax so that it can be used to "draw" patterns on the fabric, using a tool called a *tjanting*. The molten wax is held in the tjanting's bowl and it flows through a smaller hole in the nib.

The wax cools on the fabric; it prevents the dyes from coloring the fabric beneath it and spreading into other areas, allowing the rest of the fabric to be dyed. The wax is removed by ironing between sheets of newsprint.

DRAWING WITH DYES

Another method of patterning fabric, and one that isn't expensive, is drawing directly onto the fabric using fabric or silk paints and pens. When you use silk paints you should use a substance called gutta to draw the pattern first. Gutta usually comes in an easy-to-use tube, and works in a similar way to batik wax by stopping dyes spreading into each other.

The dyes can be special silk paints, ordinary fabric paints, or dyes. Food coloring also works well, but it is not colorfast, so the item cannot be washed.

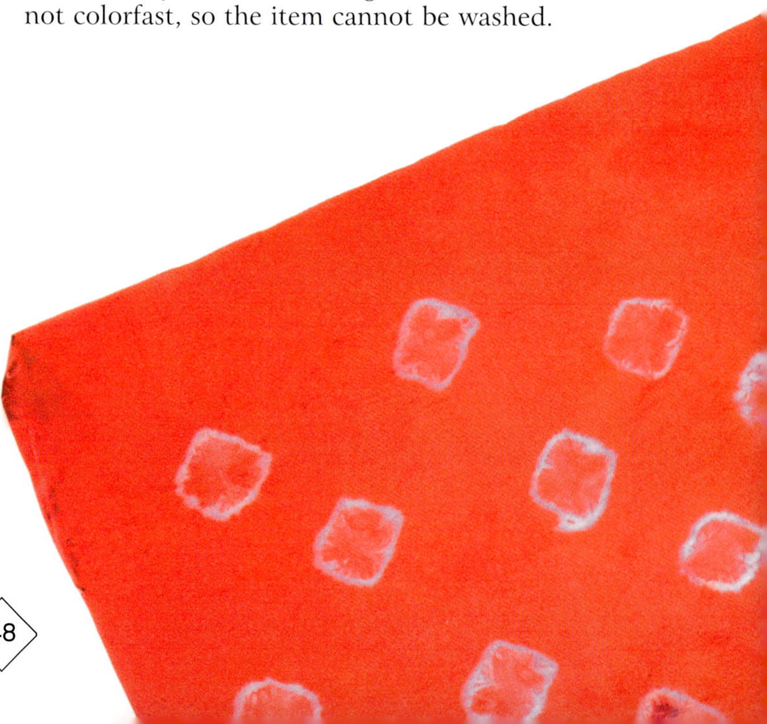

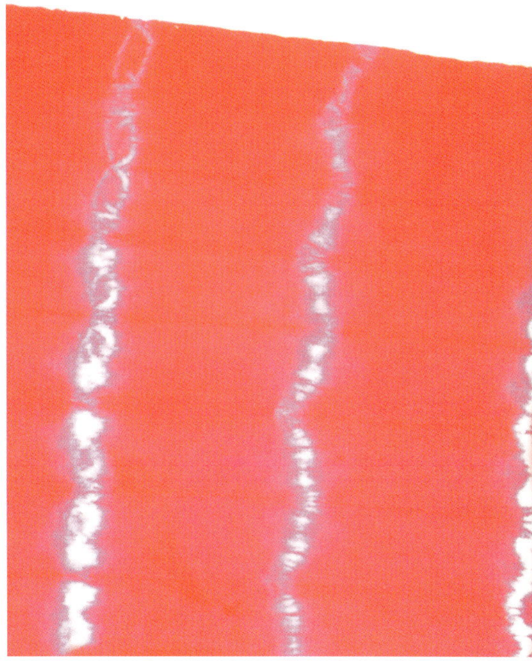

BATIK TECHNIQUE

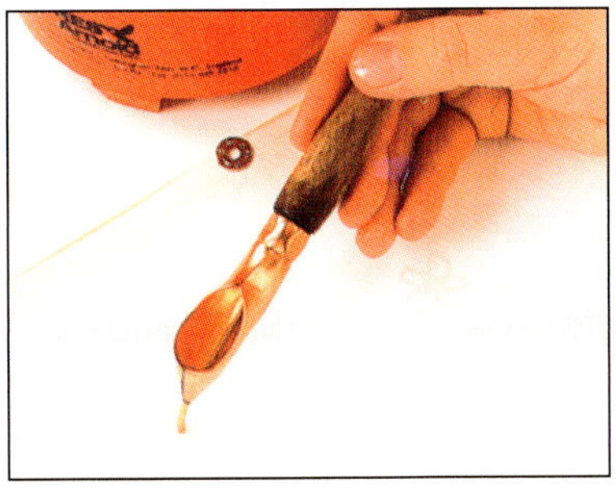

1 Once you have pinned your fabric onto a frame, use the *tjanting* to scoop up melted wax carefully from the pot. It may be useful to have a paper towel or piece of newsprint handy to wipe the nib and prevent drips as you carry it over the fabric. While the wax is still very hot, draw the pattern on the fabric with the *tjanting*.

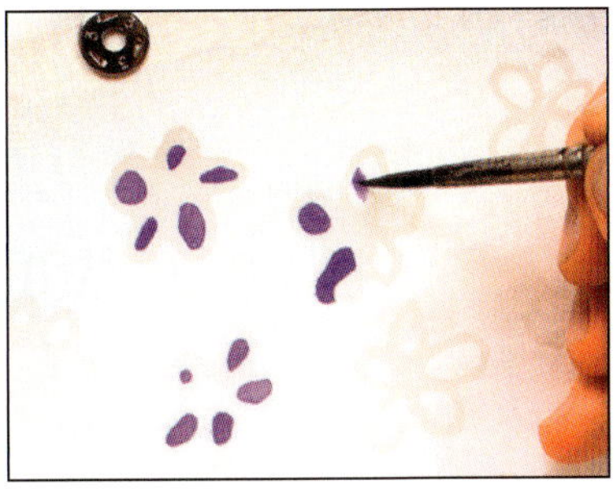

2 Once the wax has dried, the fabric can be painted. Dab the brush lightly on the fabric, allowing the dye to spread to the edges of the wax.

When using purchased dyes, it is important to read the instructions very carefully. Always cover the surrounding surfaces and your own clothes to avoid dyeing more than you want! Also, dyes can stain and irritate the skin, so it is important to wear rubber gloves.

3 The background can be painted in the same way using a thicker brush. Uneven color tones can give the fabric an interesting texture.

4 When the dye has dried, unpin the fabric from the frame and place it between several sheets of newsprint. Gently press a hot iron over the newsprint to melt the wax from the fabric.

When all the wax has melted and been absorbed into the newsprint, the fabric will feel soft again and be ready to use.

OUR CHILDREN— GROWING UP

We tend to keep all our photographs in a general family album, and as our children grow, so do the albums, bulging with a medley of pictorial records. Perhaps now is the time to take stock, edit, and select your favorite photos to put in a special scrapbook. You can reorganize your collection to create books that cover easily identifiable periods and themes, and also construct a baby's keepsake box that not only stores photographs but holds all those things that you cherish, such as a lock of hair, or a first pair of socks, or even compile a scrapbook specifically dedicated to your child's school years. The following projects you can make for your own family or give as a special present to friends.

Baby's Christening

Remember this special day in your baby's life with a book in which your guests can record their thoughts on the occasion and their wishes for your child. The beautiful personalized cover, made from raw silk and embroidered with silk ribbons, was wrapped around a blank book to make it something to treasure for itself as well as its contents. You could of course create your own design for the cover, or trace a monogram. You may also wish to include the date of your child's birth.

YOU WILL NEED

Blank pages to cover

Raw silk or other suitable fabric

Silk embroidery ribbon:
1 card each of
1/16 in. (1.3 mm) pink
1/8 in. (2.5 mm) cream
1/4 in. (5 mm) pink
1/4 in. (5 mm) cream

Stranded floss

Thread to match ribbons

Chenille needle

Tailor's chalk

Pins

Transfer (tracing) paper

Pencil

4 small pearl buttons

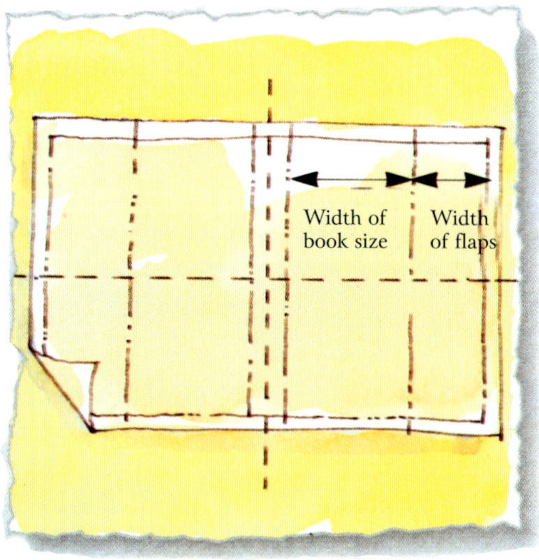

1 Measure the book, allowing for the flaps and the spine. Leave 1 in. (2.5 cm) all around for seams. Mark the fabric as shown to help you position the stitches.

2 Draw your design onto transfer paper. You can enlarge the one shown here, or use your own. To transfer the design onto the fabric prick the pattern with a pin and mark through the holes with tailor's chalk.

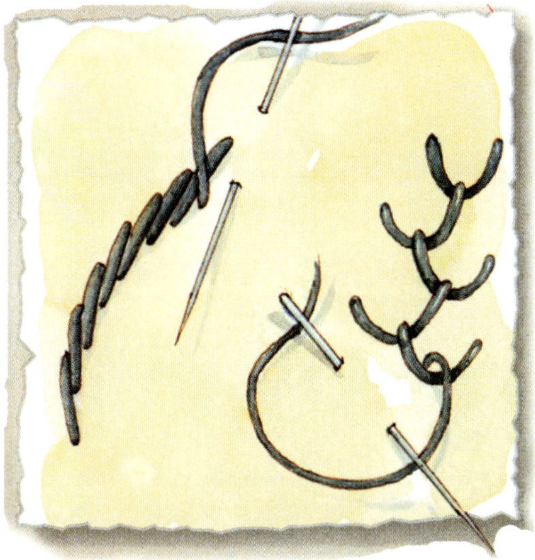

3 Using three strands of embroidery floss, work the stems and leaves with stem stitch (on the left) and feather stitch (on the right).

4 To create French knots, use three strands of embroidery floss and wrap the thread around the needle three times. Work the ribbon French knots, using the 1/16 in. (1.3 mm) pink ribbon and wrapping it around the needle only twice.

5 To make the ribbon roses, cut 14-in (35-cm) lengths of ¼-in. (5-mm) ribbon for the large ones and 10-in. (25-cm) lengths for the small ones. Using thread the same color as the ribbon, stitch large and small stars, as marked. Stitch a length of ribbon through the center of each star and weave it in and out the embroidery floss like a basket. When the rose is complete, fasten off at the back.

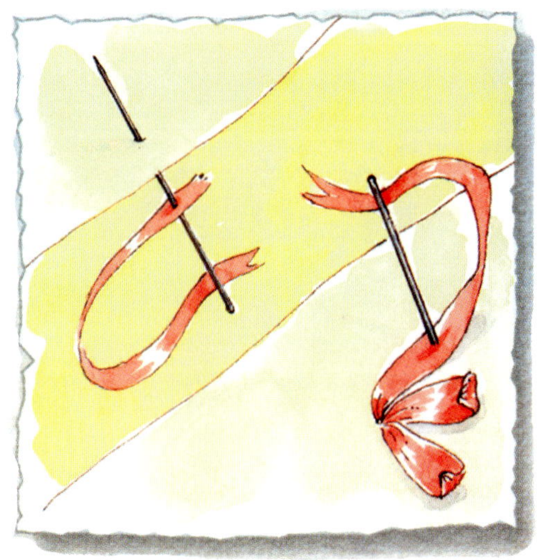

6 To make the petal flowers, stitch through the end of the ribbon into the fabric to form a soft knot on the wrong side, then allow the length of the petal and stitch through the end, guiding it with your thumb so that the ribbon sits easily in place. Fix a small pearl button to the center of each petal flower using two stitches through the fabric and tying a knot on the wrong side to secure the pearl buttons in place.

7 Embroider your chosen letter in stem stitch, then weave the ribbon in and out of the stitches, pulling it along gently.

8 When the embroidery is complete, fold the fabric right sides together and baste around two sides. Turn rightside out again and check the positioning; adjust as necessary. Turn inside out again and stitch around the two sides.

9 Turn right side out and square up the corners. Pin the hem allowance under on the open end and slipstitch in place.

10 Finally, fit the cover onto the blank pages of your book and fold the ends to form flaps. Make sure it is loose enough to allow the book to open and close, then slipstitch in place.

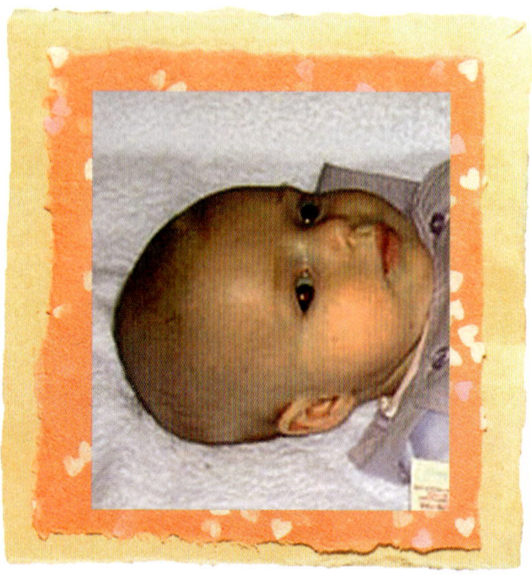

Use your own handmade paper on the inside pages to make your Christening scrapbook even more special. You can also add pockets to hold those special items you want to treasure.

Baby's Book

Here is a special book for recording those thoughts and treasured moments so that one day you can give it to your grown-up child. The unique tab closure ensures protection for the pages inside. Embellish the front cover with a papercast object to personalize your scrapbook.

YOU WILL NEED

7 sheets of white machine-made paper, *6 x 16½ in. (15 x 42 cm)*

Bone folder

Sheet of purple machine-made card, *6 x 20 in. (15 x 51 cm)*

Pencil

Ruler

Steel ruler

Craft knife

Bookbinder's needle

Waxed purple embroidery thread, *5 ft (1½ m) long*

White glue

Papercast butterfly

Set of Velcro tabs

The concertina folds consist of peaks and valleys. You may bind your book on either the peak or the valley, depending upon the look you desire. This project binds the pages on the valley. Try binding on the peak, but be sure to enlarge the front and back covers to accommodate this change.

You could make this book for a friend to record her new baby's first year. Personalize the cover with a papercast embellishment or a photograph mounted on deckle-edged handmade paper.

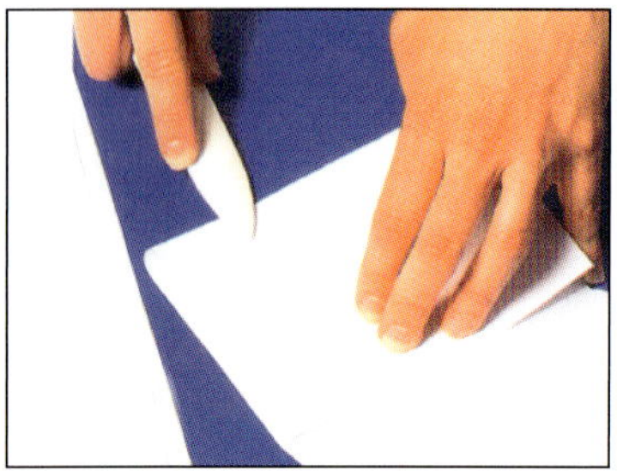

1 Fold a sheet of white machine-made paper in half widthwise, using a bone folder for a sharp crease. Open out the sheet and fold it into quarters by bringing each end to meet in the center. Fold the sheet in half and put it aside. Fold the remaining sheets in the same manner.

2 Take one folded sheet and place it on top of a sheet of purple machine-made card stock, flush with the left side of the card stock. Mark the right side of the sheet on the purple card stock with a pencil.

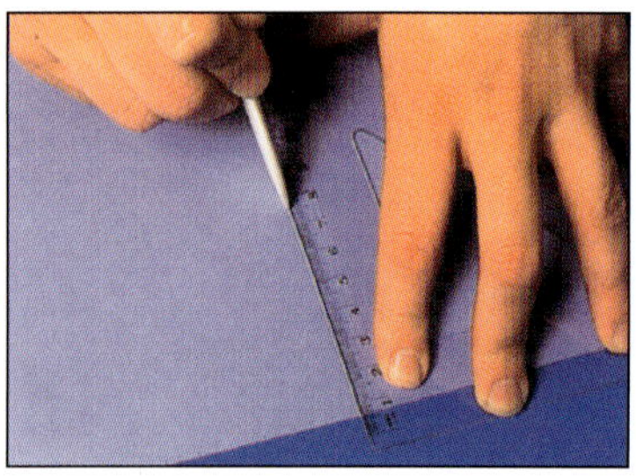

3 Make 14 additional marks to the right of this marking, on the card stock, each ⅜ in. (8 mm) apart, at the head and tail of the cover. With a ruler and bone folder, score the cover along the 15 marked points.

4 Carefully fold the card stock at the marks, alternating folding in and out to create the concertina folds of the cover.

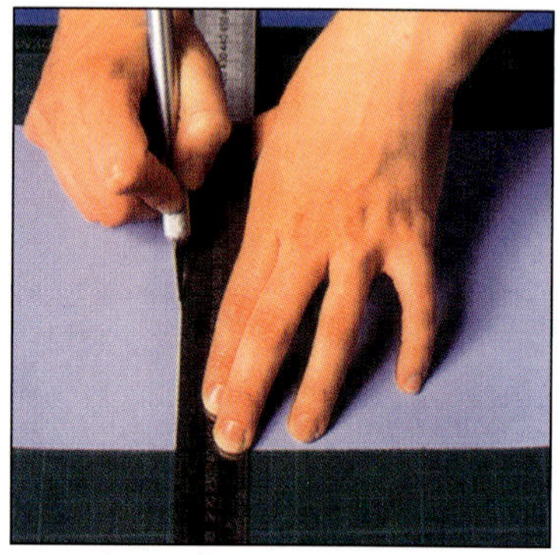

5 Measure off 4 in. (10 cm) from the back cover using a steel ruler and craft knife.

6 On the back cover piece, mark a straight line in pencil to define the back cover, 4 in. (10 cm) from the last fold of the concertina, and drawn from head to tail of the cover. On this line, measure and mark a point 2½ in. (6 cm) from the tail. Make the same two marks on the other edge of the back cover. Connect the points to form a tab, and trim using a steel ruler and craft knife.

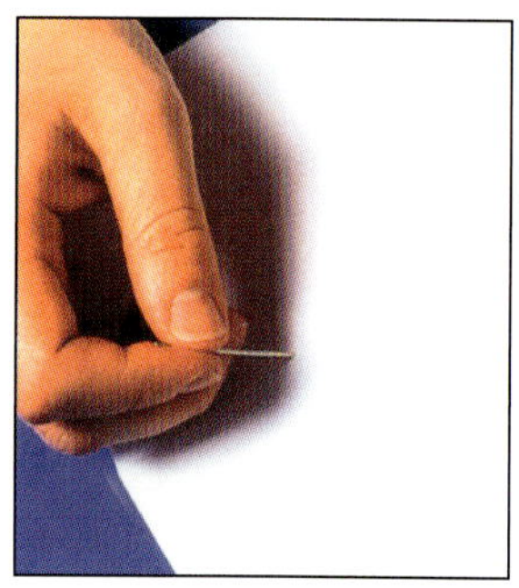

7 On each folded inner page, mark two holes, 2 in. (5 cm) apart, and 2 in. (5 cm) from the head and tail. Pierce the holes with a bookbinder's needle. Make the same markings on the valleys of the concertina folds and pierce with a bookbinder's needle.

8 Sew each folded page onto a concertina valley using a two-hole pamphlet stitch.

9 Tie a double knot on the inside of each page.

10 Apply a thin layer of white glue to the back of the papercast butterfly. Press the butterfly firmly onto the cover, and place it under a light weight for 30 minutes.

11 Trim the tab to 1½ in. (3.5 cm). Fold it over to the front cover. Attach one half of a tab of Velcro to the cover and one half to the card tab.

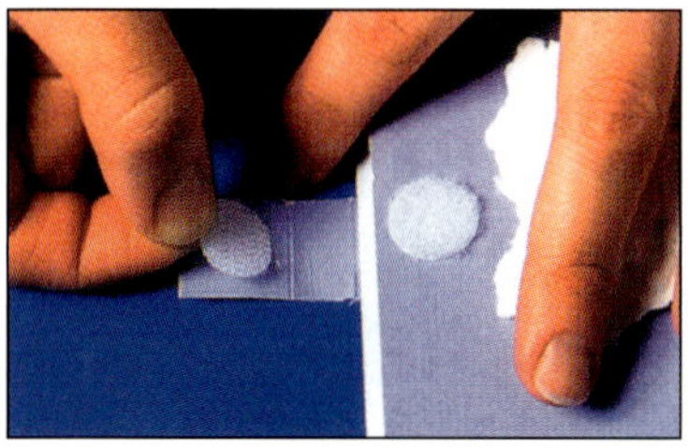

This pamphlet-style scrapbook is held together using the three-hold pamphlet stitch method.

PAMPHLET STITCH

Pamphlet stitch is one of the simplest methods of binding, and it is based on three holes. The thread can be hidden or visible as part of the design.

Pamphlet binding can be fastened together with colored embroidery thread, cord, ribbon, raffia, and even shoelaces. Select a sewing needle with a thickness similar to the thread to be used on the book. Thicker sewing materials, such as leather cord or heavy ribbon, will need a thicker needle with a larger eye. Sew a cover and inner pages together to create a quick and easy handbound book. Or create a decorative cover to be added to the section after binding.

If you want to make a larger book, simply increase the number of sewing holes to five, seven, or more, or add an extra section to give you more pages and introduce a folded cover with a pleat. If you want to keep the structure really simple, the cover need only consist of two or three folds of paper with the sewing reduced to one central hole.

The five-hole pamphlet stitch is useful for books with large pages. If the book is really big, you can increase the number of holes. Vary the distance of the holes for a different look or cut the pages into different shapes before you sew.

Book of Toys

Much as we would like to keep our children's toys, it becomes an impossible task as their playthings multiply year by year. However, we can keep records, and this scrapbook provides a way to delight your children when they are young and then amaze them when they are grown up and most of the original toys have been lost.

YOU WILL NEED

Foam board *(polyboard), 10 x 16 in. (24 x 40 cm)*

Fabric and lining fabric, *each 12 x 18 in. (30 x 45 cm)*

Fabric motif *cut with pinking shears, if desired*

Stranded floss

Thin cardboard *in different colors 6¼ x 9 in. (16 x 23 cm)*

Cloth bookbinder's tape

Ribbon

Leather punch

Choose interesting household objects to photograph for the toys to hide behind. These will also bring back memories when your child has grown up.

Choose a suitable non-stretch fabric to cover the book and salvage a motif from a favorite item of outgrown clothing for decoration.

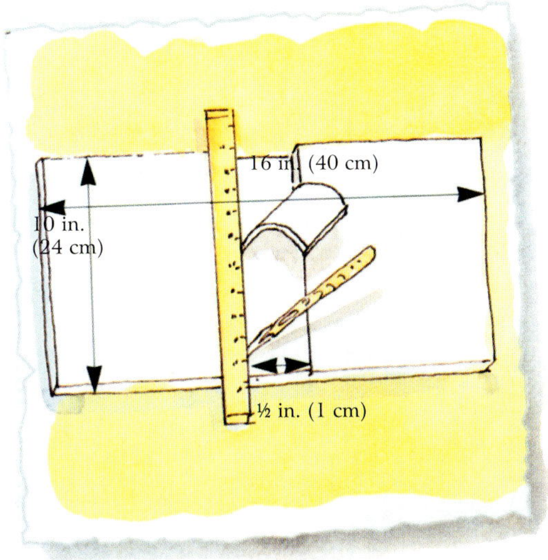

1 Cut out a rectangle of foam board (polyboard), following the diagram above. Cut partway through the board to make two parallel lines ½ in. (1 cm) apart and remove the top card and board. This gully will become the book's spine.

2 Cut out pieces of fabric and lining fabric. Place ribbon on the right side with enough to go around the book. Use stranded floss to stitch a motif from a favorite item of clothing on top of the ribbon on the right side of the fabric.

3 Place the foam board, scored side down, on the reverse side of the cover fabric. Stick two-sided tape around the perimeter of the board, slightly in from the edge. If the fabric is too bulky, snip the corners of the fabric and fold over the edges. Stick them down smoothly.

4 Turn under and press a ¼-in. (5-mm) hem on the piece of lining fabric and place it, wrong side down, on top of the foam board. It will stick to the edges of the tape not covered by the front-cover fabric. Slipstitch all around the edge to secure the inside and outside covers.

5 Cut 12 pages from different-colored cardboard and stick bookbinder's tape on both sides. The tape should overlap the edge of the page by ½ in. (1 cm). Punch nine holes through the overlapping tape with a leather punch, spacing 1 in. (2.5 cm) apart.

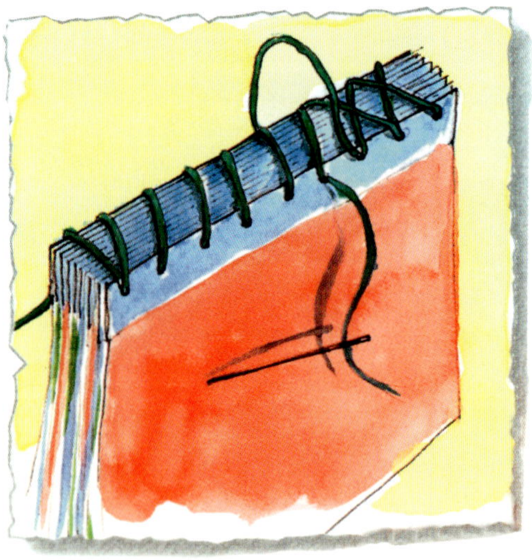

6 Using strong thread, stitch the pages together with a cross stitch and secure the ends of the thread.

7 Fold the cover inside out and use a doubled length of strong thread to stitch through the spine, connecting the stitches through the center of the cross stitches.

8 Select a toy to photograph for each page and an object for each to hide behind. Mark your foot position on the ground with chalk or masking tape and photograph each toy. Then place the object in front of the toy and take a second picture from the same position.

9 After the photos have been developed, cut out the object and attach a loop of ribbon to the right-hand edge of the back cutout. Glue a piece of matching colored paper to the back of this picture to cover the ribbon. Position the object picture over the photo of the toy and stitch to form a hinge. Affix the finished picture to the book page with glue or two-sided tape.

10 An alternative to using ribbon is to cut slits along the edge of the toy photo, place tape through the slits to the back of the toy picture, and attach the back of the object picture to the other end of the tape. Then affix the finished picture to the page in the book with glue or two-sided tape.

Memories

Although this next project is not truly a scrapbook it is a really nice way of displaying your children's photographs instead of having them hidden away in an album. This picture-frame box is a wonderful way to celebrate a special event, such as a birth, their first steps, and many other memorable occasions. Make the interior as decorative as possible and freely mix other mementos such as birth announcements or a lock of your baby's hair in with your photographs.

YOU WILL NEED

***Two-ply museum board**, for mats*

***Binder's board**, for case*

Momi paper

***Decorative papers** (mats)*

***Decorative papers** (linings)*

***Two bone clasps** (also called* tsume*)*

Grosgrain ribbon

Mylar

***Glue**, mixture, and paste*

MOMI PAPERS

A nice material to use for covering is a specific Japanese paper called *Momi*, that has the strength and the folding qualities of cloth. These papers are tough enough to be substituted for fabric, but they require special handling. The beauty of these color-saturated papers is in their crinkly surface. If the paper becomes too relaxed—for example, by the application of paste—the crinkles flatten out and the wonderful texture is lost. The solution to this problem is threefold: (1) use mixture instead of paste; (2) apply the mixture to the board rather than to the paper; and (3) don't be too aggressive with your bone folder.

GETTING STARTED

Cut the museum board to make four mats. Cut board to the desired height and width making sure that the grain runs parallel with the spine edge. Cut out the windows in the mats. The windows should be approximately ½ in. (1 cm) smaller in both height and width than the photos.

1 Cover the mats. Cut four pieces of decorative paper:
Height = height of mat plus 1½ in. (4 cm)
Width = width of mat plus 1½ in. (4 cm)

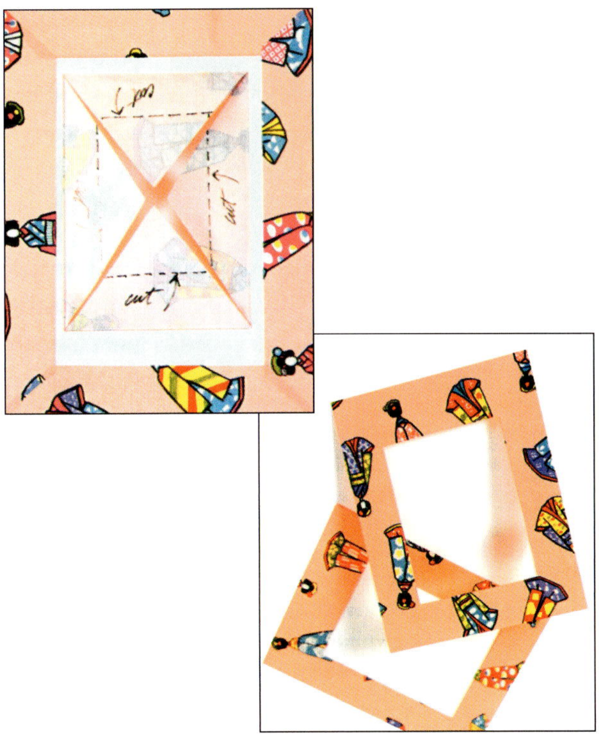

2 Paste out the paper. Center the mat on the paper and press into place. Cut the corners and finish the edges (see page 40). To finish the interior of the mat, make two diagonal cuts, from corner to corner, through the paper in the windows. Remember that wet paper tends to tear when being cut. If your paper is saturated with paste, give it a few minutes to dry before cutting.

3 Prior to pasting these flaps into position on the back of the mats, trim away excess paper with your scissors. Paste. Place the covered mats between sheets of newsprint, and under a board and weight until dry.

4 Cut the boards for the case. Cut four pieces of binder's board:
Height = height of mats plus two board thicknesses
Width = width of mats plus two board thicknesses

From your scrapboard, cut two joint spacers. Different spacers are required because, as the accordion closes, the first and last joints must accommodate more bulk than the middle joint.
Spacer 1 (for first and last joints) = two binder's board thicknesses plus two mat thicknesses plus 1/16 in. (1.3 mm).
Spacer 2 (for middle joint) = two binder's board thicknesses.

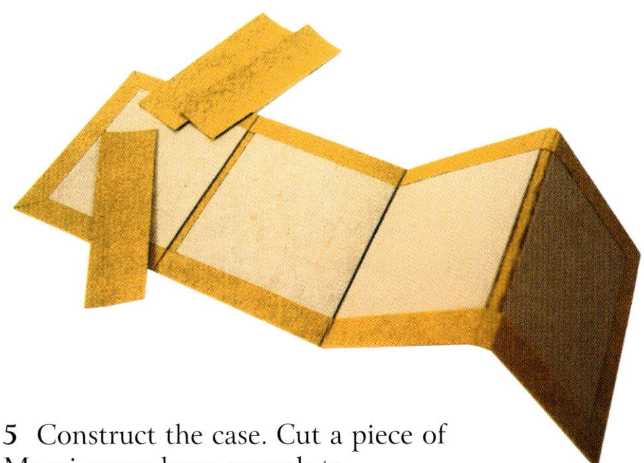

5 Construct the case. Cut a piece of Momi paper large enough to accommodate the four case boards and the joint spacers. Add a 4/5-in. (2-cm) turn-in allowance around all four edges. Brush mixture onto the case boards and gently press them into position on the paper, leaving the proper joint spaces between the boards. Cut the corners. Apply your mixture sparingly, glue the head turn-in.

6 Bring the paper onto the boards and, with the edge of your bone folder, gently press the paper into the three joints. Pinch in the paper at the corners. Repeat with tail turn-in. Complete the spine and fore edge turn-ins.

Cut three hinge strips from the Momi paper:
Height = height of case boards minus ¼ in. (0.5 cm)
Width = 2 in. (5 cm)

Stipple the mixture onto one hinge strip and, centering the strip, gently press the paper into the joints and onto the boards. Repeat with the other two hinges. Put the case aside to dry, flat, under a light weight.

7 Attach the bone clasps. Position the four mats on the case and close the case. Thread the ribbons through the slits in the bone clasps and place the clasps in the desired location on the front of the case. Mark the front of the case with four pinpricks, one on each side of the two clasps directly below their slits. (To make sure the clasps end up level with each other, make all marks on a pattern and then transfer these marks to your case.) Open up the case, remove the mats, and place the case right side up on a scrapboard. Select a chisel to match the width of your ribbons. Holding the chisel vertically, make four parallel chisel cuts (two per clasp), starting at the pinpricks and chiseling downward.

8 Angle the ends of two short pieces of ribbon and push down through the cuts, to form receiving loops for the clasps. Slide the clasps into the loops. Adjust the ribbons for a snug fit. Guide the main ribbons to the back of the case; mark for their insertion (again, with a pinprick or pattern). Make one vertical slit per ribbon.

9 Adjust the ribbons to make them taut. (Be sure the mats are inside the case as you make these adjustments.) On the inside of the case, spread the ribbon ends in opposite directions. With your knife, trace the outline of the ribbons, cutting and peeling up a shallow layer of board. Glue the ribbons into these recesses, using undiluted PVA. Make it as smooth as possible.

10 Line the case. Cut four pieces of decorative paper to fit within the case turn-ins. Paste out the papers and apply them to the case. Press the case, between newsprint and boards, under a light weight.

11 Attach the mats. The mats are glued to the case along three edges; the fourth edge is kept unglued, to allow for the insertion of the photographs. Glue backs of mats as follows:

Mat 1: Glue out the head, tail, and the long edge of the mat that will sit near the outer edge of the case (i.e. away from the joint). Use undiluted PVA, masking off areas of the mat to be kept glue free with narrow strips of paper. Brush the glue approximately ½ in. (1 cm) onto the mats. Center the mat on the case board, pressing down along the edges with your bone folder. Carefully scoop away any seeping glue with a micro-spatula.

Mats 2 and 3: Glue out the head, tail and long edge of the mat that will sit near the middle joint. Continue as with mat 1.

Mat 4: Follow the process as with Mat 1.

When all four mats have been glued to the case, press the case by placing it between newsprint and boards and under a light weight.

12 Cut four pieces of Mylar approximately 1 in. (3 cm) smaller than the mats in both height and width. Slide the Mylar under the mats. Insert photos under the Mylar.

RIGHT: *Momi papers are crinkled and are very effective when pasted down for a book cover or photo background. This series has a polished surface that makes them fairly hard-wearing, though made of woodpulp.*

Keepsake Box

Although this is not a scrapbook it is a delightful alternative to store those cherished mementos that surround the birth of a baby. It becomes a place that unites souvenirs, such as your congratulations cards, birth records, and photographs of your newborn. Because the box is covered with scented drawer lining paper, the contents are permeated with a deliciously sweet smell, making it a joy to open.

YOU WILL NEED

Foam board *(polyboard)*
Lid and base 20½ x 9 in. (52 x 23 cm)
Sides 2½ x 36 in. (6 x 91.5 cm)

Scented paper

Victorian paper scraps

Colored paper

Pressed flowers

Fastening tape

Music-box mechanism *(optional)*

The tinkling sound of the music-box mechanism inside the box will delight your child while you enjoy the contents.

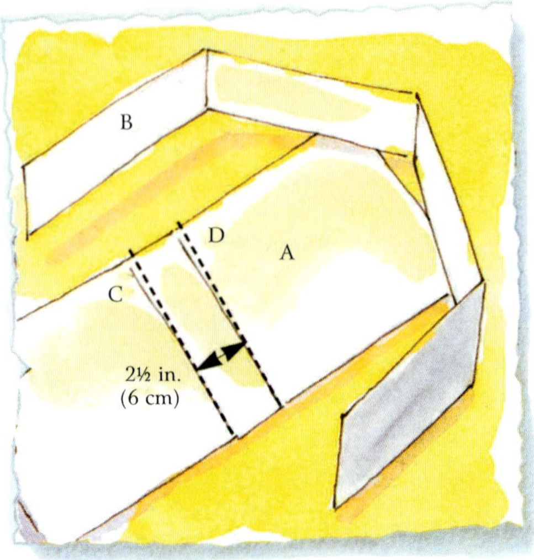

1 Cut a piece of foam board (polyboard) for the base and lid (A) and cut part way through C and D to form the spine. Cut a second piece for the sides of the box (B), divide into quarters, and cut part way through.

2 Attach a piece of scented decorative paper to the uncut side of B. Fold along the scored lines to make an open-ended cube and tape the joined edges to secure them.

3 Wrap double-sided tape around the outside of the cube you have just made. Cut a strip of scented decorative paper and use it to cover the outside of the cube.

4 Place a sheet of decorative paper wrong side up on the work surface. Spread craft (PVA) glue thinly over the cut side of A and stick the outside of the cover to the paper. Make sure the paper fits into the notches or the cover will not close properly.

5 Stick double-sided tape around the inside edges of A and fold the edges of the decorative paper onto it. Lightly stick a ribbon 2 in. (5 cm) from the edge of the inside cover. Cut a piece of decorative paper ¼ in. (5 mm) smaller than the cover and glue to the inside of the cover.

6 Glue the cube in position. Place a weight on it to hold it down evenly while it dries.

7 If you choose to use a music-box mechanism position it in a place that allows the handle to be turned. Cut a slot with a craft knife so that the handle can pass through the box. Secure the mechanism with touch-and-close fastening tape.

Make an album out of card laced together with ribbon and take a photo of your baby each month for the first year to add to the box.

8 Glue Victorian scraps to the inside lid for decoration. Choose ones that are appropriate to the birth theme, such as a stork carrying a baby or bunches of flowers.

9 Make a plaque to decorate the front. Here we have used pressed flowers and a photograph surrounded by layers of deckle-edged papers in various colors, and borders of Victorian scraps. Assemble the layers as you wish and stick them together with double-sided tape. Glue the plaque to the outside of the lid and decorate the inside of the lid with more Victorian scraps. Fill the box with treasured memories.

Artist's Portfolio

By making a scrapbook that contains your child's own paintings and drawings, you not only present him or her with a delightful toy, but you also encourage him in a very worthwhile pastime. Children love to look back at their outgrown works of art, and this book will be a valuable record of their progress as well as a source of pleasure throughout their childhood and beyond.

Choose paintings that you particularly like, or ones that mark key developmental stages.

YOU WILL NEED

Canvas *or other heavyweight fabric, enough for 6 pieces of 22¾ x 14 in. (57 x 35 cm)*

Needle and strong thread

Stranded floss

Batting (wadding)

Bias binding*, 3 colors of ½ in. (1 cm) wide x 73½ in. (184 cm)*

Mementos and photocopies of child's art

Fabric tape and ribbon *(optional)*

Sewing machine *(optional)*

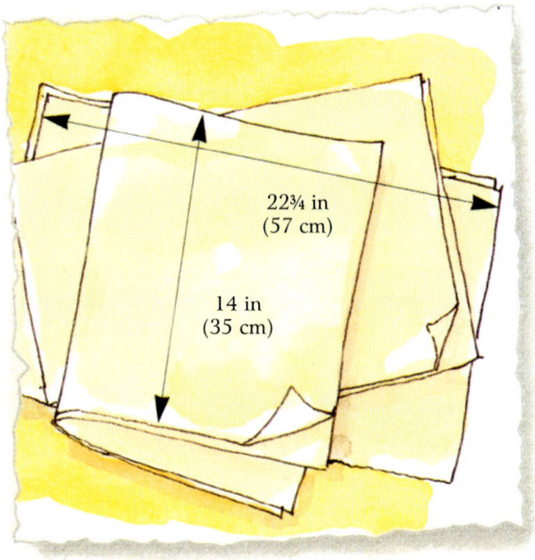

1 Cut six pieces of fabric, each measuring 22¾ x 14 in. (57 x 35 cm). On the cover piece, embroider your child's name, date, and any other decoration you wish.

2 Cut three pieces of batting (wadding) 22¾ x 14 in. (57 x 35 cm) and sandwich one piece between two pieces of fabric, with wrong sides toward the batting. Baste the layers together, working out from the center to keep distortion to a minimum. Then baste around the edges.

3 Cut three lengths of differently colored bias binding. Each double page will need a 73½-in. (184-cm) length of ½-in. (1-cm) wide bias binding. Apply bias binding along the raw edges of each double page by hand or machine. Repeat to make three double pages.

4 Select mementos and arrange your photocopied or original art in a pleasing display. Stitch the chosen items in place, making sure you do not stitch through to the other side.

5 Stack the pages in order, with the cover page on the bottom, and stitch through the center fold, using strong thread to create a spine.

6 To hang the book, stitch a loop of fabric tape to the top of the spine. If the book is very bulky, you can tie it closed with a pretty ribbon. Store with sheets of tissue paper between the pages to protect the surface of the pictures.

A book like this would be a delightful present to make for Father's or Mother's Day.

ROMANTIC KEEPSAKES

When you are old and gray and full of sleep,
And nodding by the fire, take down this book,
And slowly read, and dream of the soft look
Your eyes had once, and of their shadows deep.

How many loved your moments of glad grace,
And loved your beauty with love false or true;
But one man loved the pilgrim soul in you,
And loved the sorrows of your changing face.

And bending down beside the glowing bars
Murmur, a little sadly, how love fled
And paced upon the mountains overhead
And hid his face amid a crowd of stars.

W. B. Yeats

A Lover's Album

Remnants of luscious lavender, purple, and peach materials have been brought together to form this richly textured album. The simple binding uses post fittings—available from specialist suppliers—which allow pages to be added or removed.

YOU WILL NEED

Sheet of stiff cardboard, *20 x 15 in. (50 x 38 cm)*

Open-weave gauze bandage

Craft glue (PVA)

Silk for cover, *30 x 12 in. (80 x 30 cm)*

Lining fabric, *30 x 12 in. (80 x 30 cm)*

Square of velvet, *5 in. (13 cm)*

Lightweight iron-on interfacing, *15 x 12 in. (38 x 30 cm)*

Patch of fabric, *6 x 7 in. (15 x 18 cm)*

Strip of webbing

Embroidery thread

2 squares of batting *¼ in. (6 mm) thick: 9½ in. (24 cm) square and 5 in. (13 cm) square*

Star sequin

Double-sided carpet tape

Card stock

5 A1 sheets of card *for stock pages*

2 endpapers, *10 x 12 in. (25.5 x 30.5 cm)*

Scissors

Photographic metal mounting posts with screw heads

1 Cut two squares from the cardboard sized 10 x 10 in. (25 x 25 cm) and two strips 10 x 1½ in. (25 x 4 cm). Pair up each strip with a square. Join them together by glueing a length of open-weave bandage across them using craft glue, leaving a ¼ in. (6 mm) gap in between.

2 Cut out two rectangles of fabric for the outside covers sized 15 x 12 in. (38 x 30 cm) and two for the inside cover 9¾ x 14¾ in. (24.5 x 42.5 cm). Cut the square of velvet into a heart shape. Back each piece with iron-on interfacing and iron as directed.

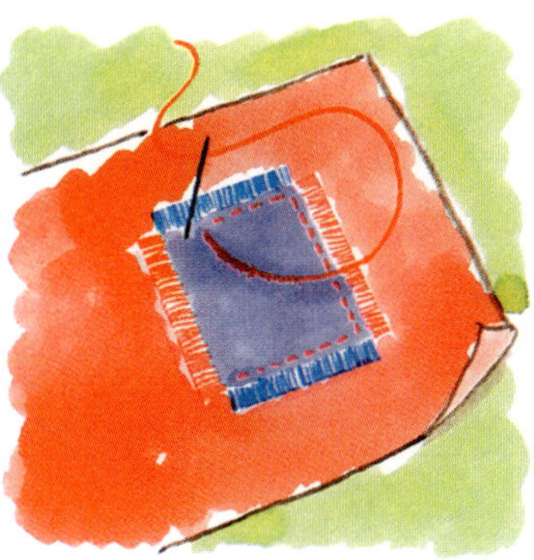

3 Take the patch of fabric and fray the edges by about ½ in. (1 cm). Using the webbing, iron it onto the middle of the cover fabric. Stitch round it using embroidery thread.

4 Take the velvet heart as a guide and cut out a heart shape from the smaller square of batting. Using running stitch, sew the heart to the cover, sandwiching the batting.

5 Using a fine beading needle and a simple stitch, sew the sequins to the heart. Secure them with a small bead. Space them evenly around the patch.

6 Pad the cover using the larger square of batting. Spread a thin layer of craft glue over the cover interfacing and lay the batting in position. The heart should be central to the wadding. Smooth any creases along the strip end.

7 Carefully turn the cover over. Stick double-sided carpet tape around the edge of the inside cover. Trim off corners and cut away the joint between the cover and the spine. Fold in edging, attaching it to the tape, making sure the cover is taut and even. Repeat on the other cover.

9 Using a leather punch, create holes evenly spaced along the cover strip 6 in. (15 cm) apart. Cut out about 20 sheets of card stock 11 x 9½ in. (28 x 24 cm). Score a margin 1½ in. (4 cm) in each and turn them in. Punch holes ¾ in. (2 cm) in from the edge 6 in. (15 cm) apart to match the cover.

8 Once the covers are dry you can line them with fabric. Spread craft glue over the lining fabrics and position the covers carefully. Ensure you smooth out any creases with a bone folder. While the books are drying, place a medium-weight book over them to keep them flat.

10 Cut two 9½-in. (24-cm) square endpapers (reinforce the holes if necessary). Insert the metal mounting posts through the holes on the inside of the base cover. Then fold over the margin strip. Thread the endpaper on first followed by the pages, and finally the front endpaper. Put on the cover, fit the screw heads to secure it, and fold the back cover.

Once the screws have been undone from this post-bound album, you can add or take away pages of your choice.

Valentine's Day

Sew any number of beads, buttons, bells, and bows onto bright-colored plastic canvas to make a special Valentine Scrapbook. The outside looks like a conventional book, but untie the ribbon and you find heart-shaped pages with a deckle-edge onto which you can stencil motifs, or stick pictures or special mementos that reflect the romance of Valentine's Day.

YOU WILL NEED

Sheet of pink plastic embroidery canvas with an integral tag *(or hanging hook)*

Stranded floss

Satin ribbon

Colored felt and foam

Colored beads, hearts, and bells

Craft paper *(in pink, red, and mauve)*

Deckle-edge scissors

Heart, flower, and alphabet stencils and stencil paint and brush *(optional)*

Paper brad fastener

1 Fold the plastic canvas in half with the tag at the back. Decorate the cover by sewing or glueing on decorations with a Valentine theme. You could use simple shapes cut from felt or foam, or from old magazines or wrapping paper.

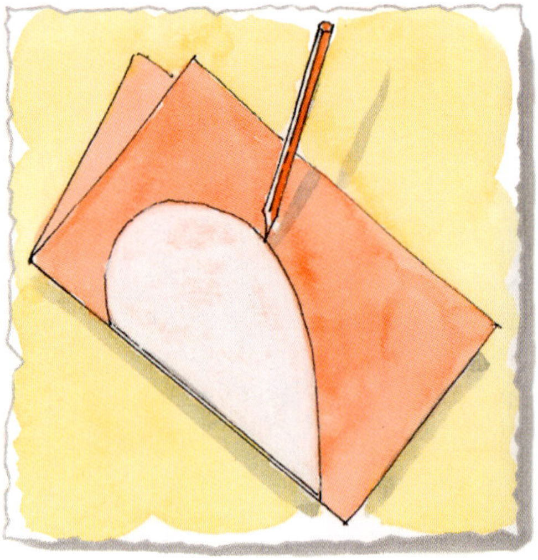

2 To make a template for the pages, fold a sheet of paper in half and draw half a heart shape on it. Cut it out and use it to make additional pages. Use deckle-edge scissors for a festive look.

3 Cut two small foam hearts in different colors and push a paper brad fastener through them. Secure the fastener to the front of the cover in line with the tag at the back.

4 Tie a length of ribbon on to the tag, with one end longer than the other. Tie a double-knotted bow so it won't unravel, and twist the long end over the brad to close the folder.

5 Hold the pages in place with a length of ribbon tied around the spine of the book. Tie a bow on the outside of the cover and secure the ribbon in position with the aid of a brad or a few decorative stitches.

This album can be your own secret record, to store somewhere safe from prying eyes. Decorate the pages with heart and rose motifs. Use it to keep your own cards, or give it to a lover, with special messages written inside.

Embossed Wedding Album

Embossing with embossing liquid is easy, although it requires patience and a steady hand. To gain confidence, draw out your pattern and pipe over the lines, progressing to working freehand. Embossing liquid responds best to a continuous flowing movement, so maintain an even pressure, rather than stopping and starting. The liquid smudges easily, so let each area of pattern dry.

YOU WILL NEED

Post-bound album

Sheet of card stock

***Embossing liquid** in pearlized silver, pink, green, and mauve*

Pencil

Scissors

Craft knife

Deckle-edge scissors

1 Make a heart template by folding a sheet of card stock in half and drawing the shape before cutting. Unscrew the album and remove a page. Draw round the heart shape onto the page.

2 Pierce the center of the heart with a craft knife. Insert the deckle-edge scissors through the hole and snip about 1 in. (2.5 cm) in from the edge to get a pretty border.

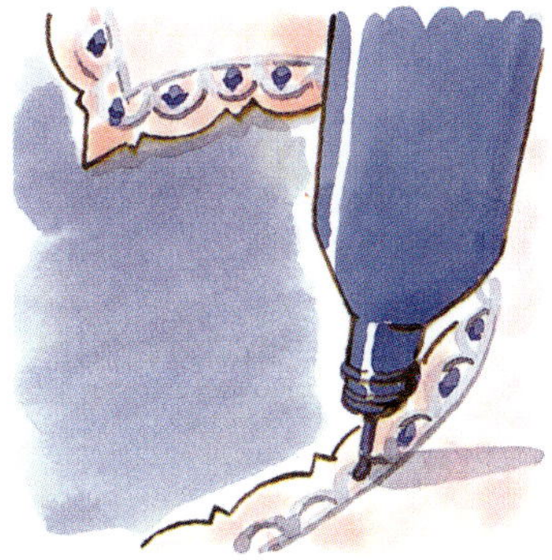

3 Pipe a ¼ in. (6 mm) line around the heart with the pearlized silver embossing liquid. Leave to dry. Using the same liquid, make a scalloped edge along this line and then add dots to each scallop. Leave to dry.

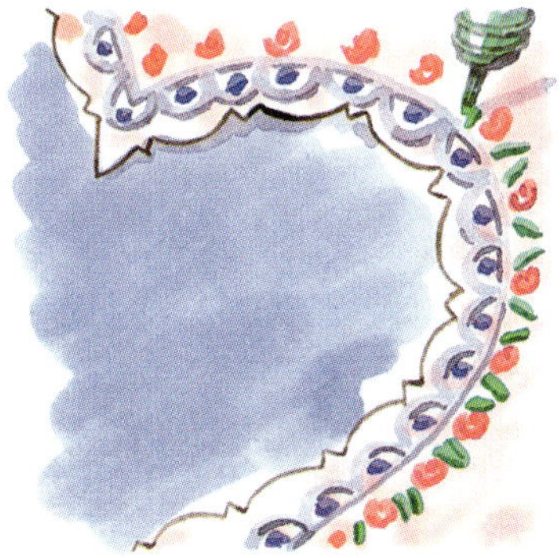

4 To create a rosebud effect, make a small spiral with the pearlized pink fluid at every scallop interval. Leave to dry before piping in the pearlized green leaves.

5 Decorate each corner with groups of three rosebuds, stylized leaves, and silver corner tabs. Leave to dry.

6 Add broad scrolls in each corner. Finish by adding a dotted border of delicate pearlized mauve dots.

LEFT: *Cut the card stock with deckle-edge scissors to make a romantic mount for your special photograph. Decorate it with piped patterns using embossing liquid or metallic embossing powder (right).*

VARIATION

1 To create a picture frame, measure the size of the picture you wish to frame. Decide on the depth of the frame and draw both inner and outer lines with a ruler and pencil. The distance between the lines should be about 1 in. (2.5 cm). Cut the frame out along the pencil line using deckle-edge scissors. To create a decorative inner edge, pierce the center of the paper using a scalpel, and cut along the pencil line with a different pair of deckle blades.

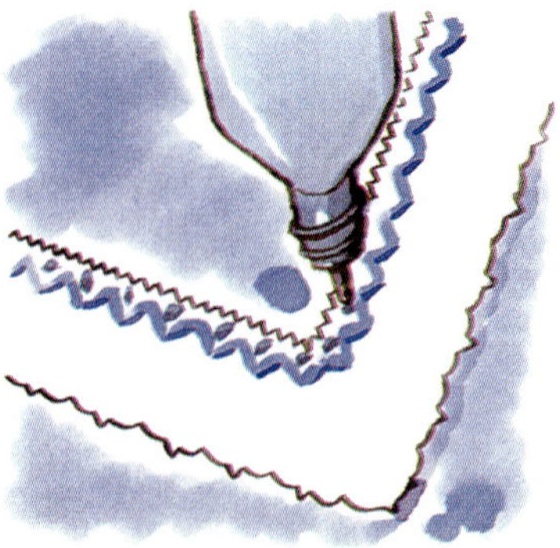

2 Using pearlized mauve embossing liquid, pipe a border around the inner frame. Allow to dry. Add silver dots between the scallops.

3 Add stylized rosebuds along the outer edge and leave to dry. Join the rosebuds to the inner edge with pearlized green stems. Leave to dry.

4 All around the border add pearlized silver crosses between each rosebud. Position the photograph in the frame and stick in place with photo corners. Return the page to the album and tighten the screws.

RIGHT: *Create tailor-made photographic mounts in the shape and color of your choice. Here, a cherished wedding photograph is enhanced by deckle-edging and embossing, two simple techniques that will add that individual touch. Practice first on a piece of paper so that you can avoid any messy errors.*

Wedding Memories

Whether you are making this book as a gift for a friend or family member, or for your own cherished memories, it will be a pleasure to produce this more traditional album with its pretty details, beautiful fabric, and satin roses and ribbons.

YOU WILL NEED

Blank hardback book or album

Plain cotton fabric

Batting (wadding)

Patterned fabric

Gold-colored paper or lightweight cardboard

Extra paper to decorate inside *(optional)*

Ribbons, roses, pearl beads, and other trims

Fabric scissors

Deckle-edge scissors

Pins

You start with an everyday book or album and add an extra-special touch by covering it with beautiful fabric and completing the effect with a colorful bouquet of satin roses and ribbons that complement the bride's choice of theme.

1 Measure the book and cut the plain cotton fabric, as shown, to cover it. Cut batting (wadding) to fit the inside front cover. Cut the patterned fabric to fit the outside front cover and hold both in place on the plain fabric with pins.

2 Stitch the batting (wadding) and patterned fabric to the plain fabric, catching in ribbon ties along the edges as you work. Glue the edges of the cover over onto the inside of the book, stretching it taut but allowing enough give to bend the book at the spine.

3 Glue the first and last pages of the book to the inside cover to hide the edges of the fabric. If you wish, glue gold paper to the inside covers. Stitch a cluster of ribbons, roses, beads, and other trims, and sew them onto the front cover.

INSIDE IDEAS

Cut out hearts from colored tissue paper or gold paper to border the photographs.

Cut a heart out of a page preceding a group photo, so that the newlyweds are looking through—then the next page reveals the larger group.

Crop photos with deckle-edge scissors to decorate plain pages.

Stick pieces of confetti from your special day on the page.

Dry petals from your bouquet and stick these into your wedding scrapbook.

Honeymoon Heaven

Not many people think of making a special book dedicated to their honeymoon photos and memorabilia, but this book with its layers of delicate organza and Indian mirror decorations is transformed into a precious memento. To close the book, thread a ribbon through a slot in the spine and tie it in a bow.

YOU WILL NEED

Blank hardback book or album

5 organza pieces *in different colors*

Craft glue (PVA)

Ribbon *½ in. (1.5 cm) wide, 24 in. (61 cm) long*

Indian mirror decorations, sequins, beads, or flat-backed buttons

Small envelope

Double-sided carpet tape

Ruler

Scissors

Scalpel

Bone folder

1 Measure the cover of the book and cut three pieces of organza to fit, each in a slightly smaller size.

2 Fray the ends of each piece by pulling away the cross-threads of the cloth.

3 Spread a thin coat of craft glue over the cover of the book. Lay on the largest piece of organza and smooth out. Repeat with the other two sheets of organza. Leave to dry.

4 On the inside cover, use a scalpel to cut a lengthwise slot midway along the spine fold, at least as wide as the ribbon. Cut only through the cover and not into the stitching. Repeat at the back.

5 Thread the ribbon from the inside front cover over the outside spine and in through the back. You will need enough to wrap around your book once and tie with a generous bow.

6 Using craft glue, stick the ribbon to the inside front cover. When dry, repeat at the back.

7 Open the book and cut two organza rectangles to fit across the width of the inside front and back pages and covers. These will be the endpapers.

8 Glue the first piece of organza onto the inside back cover only, allowing enough give to enable the book to open or close. Press along the spine fold with a bone folder and smooth out any creases. Leave to dry. Repeat on inside front cover.

9 Glue decorations in place on the front cover with craft glue. Leave to dry.

10 Attach an attractive envelope to the inside front page with double-sided carpet tape.

Fine organza has been pasted down to make sumptuous endpapers and a silver envelope is added to keep small mementos safe.

Golden Wedding

Two gold-colored cake boards or covered foam boards have been used to make the cover of this book. Greeting cards, such as the heart-shaped cutout that frames the couple cutting their anniversary cake in this project, provide an inexpensive way to decorate the front cover. Inside the album, delicate lace doilies look lovely bordering old black-and-white wedding photographs.

Embossed borders especially suit old photos. These edges can be colored with felt-tip pens, echoing those hues in the tinted photos.

YOU WILL NEED

Foam board *(polyboard)*

2 gold-colored *12-in. (30-cm) square cake boards or 2 12-in. (30-cm) square foam boards covered with gold-leaf wrapping paper*

Gold paper

Bookbinder's tape

Light-colored card

Glassine paper

Cord

Clear sheet of acetate 4 x 5 in. *(10 x 12 cm)*

Old greeting cards

Hole punch

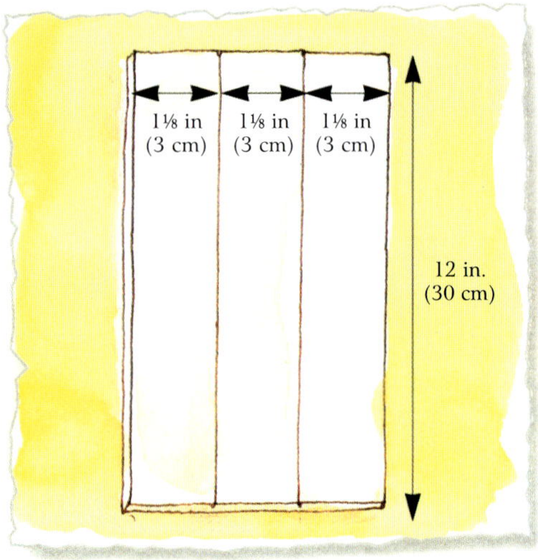

1 Cut a piece of foam board 3¾ x 12 in. (9 x 30 cm) and cut two parallel lines partway through, placed an equal distance from the sides—1¼ in. (3 cm). Fold along the cut lines to make the spine of the album.

2 Cut a sheet of gold paper 4½ x 12½ in. (11 x 32 cm) and glue it to the outside (cut side) of the spine, making sure the paper fits into the cut recesses. Fold the paper over onto the inside of the spine, overlapping all the edges.

3 Lay the spine flat and place a cake board or gold-leaf-covered foam board square on each side, wrong sides up, leaving a gap of ¼ in. (5 mm), as shown.

4 Place a ½ in. (1cm) wide strip of gold paper face down to cover the gaps. Tape in place.

5 Cut a rectangle of gold paper 12 x 28 in. (30 x 71 cm) and glue it to the inside of the cover. Smooth out any bubbles or wrinkles. Set aside to dry.

6 Reinforce the hinged section with white bookbinder's tape—here it has been deckle-edged to give it a decorative effect. Pierce two holes, 3 in. (7.5 cm) apart, along the front and back of the spine section.

7 Cut out 20 or more sheets of paper approximately 11 x 13 in. (28 x 33 cm) and deckle-edge them. Score a line 1¼ in. (3 cm) from the edge of one side and fold over.

8 Cut sheets of glassine paper 10 x 12 in. (25 x 30 cm) and fit one into each fold, then glue the fold shut. Use a hole punch to make two holes 3 in. (7.5 cm) apart.

9 Thread cord through the holes on the back cover, thread the pages onto the cord, and thread the cord through the front-cover holes. Tie the ends of the cord in a decorative bow.

10 Stick a photograph and cut-out card, as shown, on the front cover, using two-sided tape. If using a photo, as I have, place a piece of protective acetate over the image.

The edging for this picture has been embossed and stamped in silver.

Here is another idea for a scrapbook cover using a combination of different fabrics. The stitching in highlight colors cleverly emphasizes the repeat motifs, which makes it very effective and eye-catching.

HOLIDAY SOUVENIRS

This section looks at different ways of preserving your holiday souvenirs and memories. Ask your family and friends to keep the postcards that you send them over the years so that you can put them all together and bring back the joys of all the places you have visited. Relive the sounds of the sea by placing seashells, pieces of dried seaweed, and any other pieces you have picked up off the beach. Use these inspirational scrapbooks and boxes as a pick-me-up—just open them up on those gray, cold days of winter and remember the warm days of summer.

Postcard Box

Our first project in this section is not a scrapbook, but it is an ideal way of storing your postcards. Over the years you have probably hoarded travel postcards of places both seen and unseen. Quite apart from the memories or dreams they evoke, picture postcards are cheap miniature works of art.

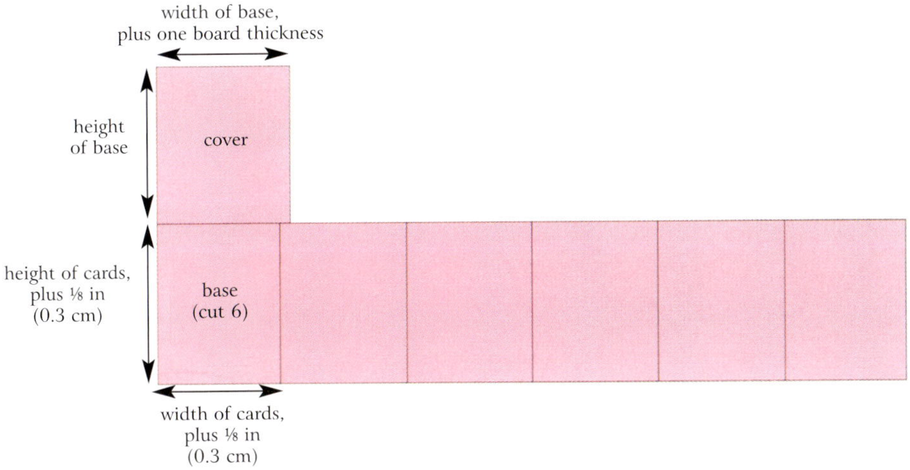

1 Cut out all of the boards, following the layout above. Cut six pieces to:
Height = height of postcards plus ⅛ in. (0.3 cm)
Width = width of postcards plus ⅛ in. (0.3 cm)

Remember: grain must run from head to tail. Label one piece "base," and set it aside. Label one piece "fore-edge flap," and set it aside. Cut one piece in half, crosswise; trim a sliver off each piece, crosswise. Label these boards "head flap" and "tail flap," and set them aside.

Cut two 2-in. (5-cm) deep strips off one of the remaining boards, crosswise. Label these boards "head wall" and "tail wall." Cut a lengthwise strip, 2 in. (5 cm) plus one board thickness in width, from one of the remaining boards. Label it "fore-edge wall." From the last remaining board cut a lengthwise strip that measures 2 in. (5 cm) plus two board thicknesses in width. Label it "spine wall." If you wish to make a shallower or deeper box, adjust the depth of these walls accordingly. You have now used up all six pieces. The final board, the cover board, is cut separately. Cut a board to:
Height = height of base board
Width = width of base board plus one board thickness

Label this piece "cover." From a leftover board, cut a narrow strip a scant two board thicknesses in width (grain long for ease in cutting). This will be your joint spacer. You need only one spacer; it will be reused several times.

YOU WILL NEED

Binder's board *(60 point)*

Bookcloth

Decorative paper

Elastic cord

1 button *(or more, for decorating)*

1 postcard or photograph

Sewing thread

PVA, mixture, and paste

Pressure-sensitive adhesive

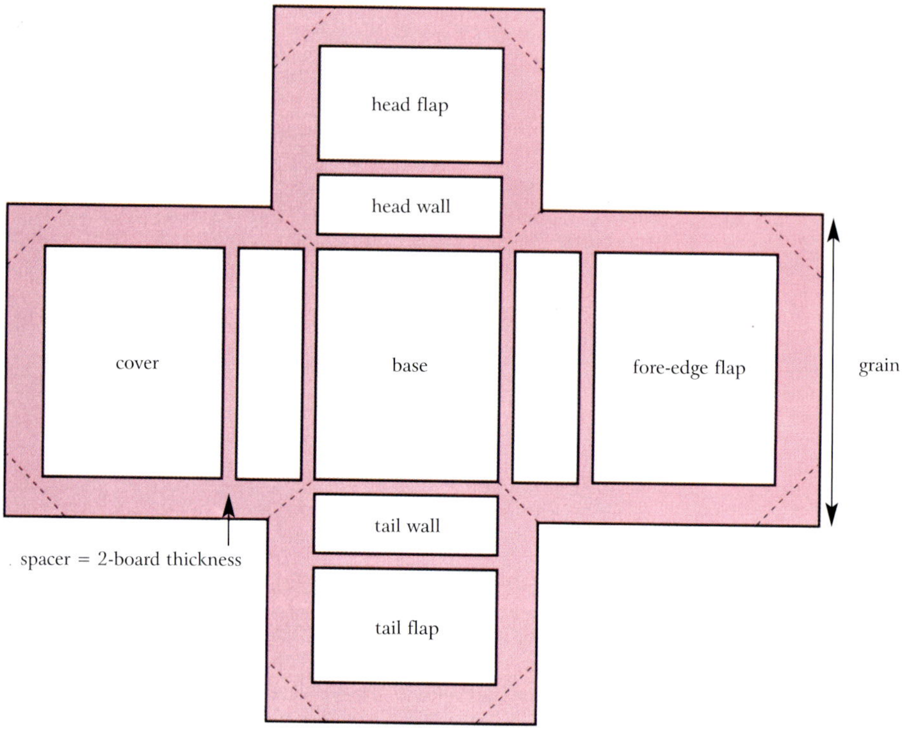

2 Cut a piece of bookcloth large enough to accommodate all of the boards with a generous margin. This box requires a piece of cloth approximately 22 in. (56 cm) square. Trim off the selvage, or bound edge, of the cloth. Do not trim any other cloth until the boards have been glued into place.

Glue the boards onto the cloth. Place the cloth, wrong side up, on newsprint. Arrange the boards on the cloth, making sure the grain direction of the cloth and the board is the same. On a separate stack of newsprint, glue the boards one at a time and press them onto the cloth. The same spacer will be used between all of the boards (see drawing above). Start with the cover board and work your way across the horizontal plane before glueing the vertical elements. When all of the boards are in place, turn the cloth over and rub down with your bone folder to make sure no air bubbles remain.

Trim the turn-in margins. Cut a scrap board to approximately ¾ in (2 cm). Use it to trace around the edges of the boards, drawing the turn-in allowance. Slide a cutting mat under the cloth and trim, using a knife and straight-edge.

3 Cut the cloth at the four corners of the base board, slicing diagonally through the turn-in, cutting in as close as possible to the tip of the board. Cut off the (eight) triangles at the outer corners of the boards. Stay 1½ board thicknesses away from the tip of the boards.

4 Glue the turn-ins. Start with the eight turn-ins that touch the walls; finish with the four turn-ins that land on the flaps. Use your ½ in. (1 cm) brush. Before glueing, slip narrow strips of grain newsprint under each turn-in. Glue. Remove the waste strip and press the cloth against the board edge. With the edge of your bone folder, work the cloth into the two joints, pressing back and forth until the fabric has stuck. With the broad side of your bone folder, press the cloth onto the boards. Work through a waste sheet to prevent marking the cloth.

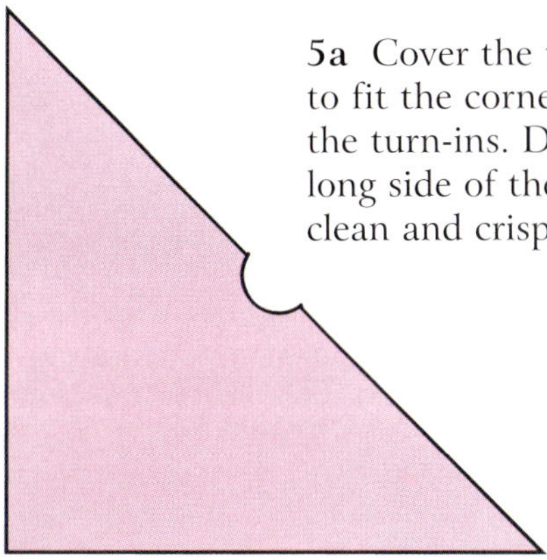

5a Cover the tips of the base board. Cut four triangles from the fabric off-cuts and trim them to fit the corners of the base board. They should match up with, and complete, the edges of the turn-ins. Do not overlap the fabric. If necessary, scoop out a slight crescent shape along the long side of the triangle to keep the right angle formed by the vertical and horizontal planes clean and crisp.

Allow a 4/5 in. (2 cm) margin of cloth around all board edges. Reserve the leftover bits of fabric for finishing details. This box requires a piece of cloth approximately 22 in. (56 cm) square.

5b Glue out one triangle. Press it lightly onto the base board. Immediately work the fabric into the two joints, pressing back and forth with your bone folder.

5c Mold the cloth around the tip of the board, patting down any loose threads. Repeat with the other three triangles.

6a Decorate the box. This is the box's best moment: When you choose a card and a handful of buttons and make your box an object of delight. Design the cover. Include in your design one button that will be the box's closure. If affixing a photograph or a postcard, use a pressure-sensitive adhesive to adhere the artwork to the cover; eventually, the card will be sewn into place. Arrange the button(s) on the cover. Punch holes through the boards to correspond with the button holes. Sew on the button(s).

6b Note: If not incorporating buttons into your design, punch holes through the card in strategic places—the corners, for example—and stitch the card in place. The pressure-sensitive adhesive is not secure enough for permanent attachment. Punch two holes in the fore-edge wall for the elastic cord. Thread both ends of the cord through the holes; adjust cord for the proper tension. If desired, thread a button or two onto the cord, to disguise these holes. Cut two shallow channels in the board and tip down the ends of the cord using undiluted PVA. Be persistent: The elastic does not want to stick! Press with your folder to flatten the cord. One or two careful hits with a hammer sometimes does the trick.

7a Cover the inside walls. Cut four strips of cloth from your leftovers. These strips will extend from the base board to the flaps, covering the walls. They are cut to fit approximately one board thickness away from the outer edges of the box. Cut two strips for the spine and fore-edge walls:
Height = height of walls minus two board thicknesses
Width = depth of walls plus 2 in. (5 cm)

Cut two strips for the head and tail walls:
Height = depth of wall plus 2 in. (5 cm)
Width = width of walls minus two board thicknesses

7b Grain should run from head to tail. Glue out the spine wall covering. Position the cloth on the base board, even with the turn-ins and centered heightwise. With the edge of your bone folder, quickly press the cloth into the joint nearest the base; smooth the cloth across the spine wall; press it into the second joint; smooth the cloth onto the cover board. Repeat with the other three wall coverings.

8 Line the box. Cut five pieces of paper to line all panels of the box. These papers are cut to fit approximately one board thickness away from all four edges.

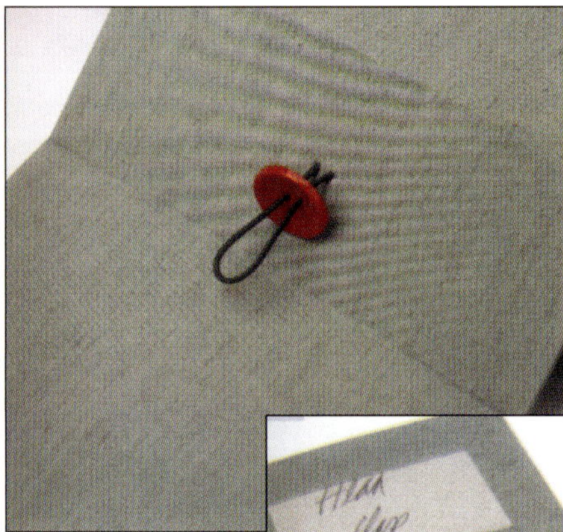

RIGHT: *This scrapbook was covered in paper that was previously stained with tea to "age" it, so that it was in keeping with a collection of old family seaside keepsakes and postcards. The fretwork front cover was inspired by decorative nineteenth-century ironwork found on piers and seafront buildings.*

BELOW *Inside this scrapbook is a collage of photographs, watercolor sketches, postcards, tickets, and labels that built up a story of the person's trip to France. The front cover was made up from an old cheese box which was decorated with seashore finds.*

Holiday Journal

Do you keep a journal of your memories while on holiday? Here is a way to decorate the cover with collage made from some of your mementos—why not use a thin piece of wood as the base on which to stick your finds and attach an envelope to store those smaller treasures.

1 Tear out a page from your notebook and use the holes to mark out spaces around the edge of the front and back covers.

2 Using a punch, make holes all the way round the two covers.

3 Tie a knot in the end of a length of raffia. Thread from the inside corner next to the spine and oversew all round the cover edges, including the spine edge. Secure with a knot on the inside when complete.

4 Tear the fine colored paper into small pieces. Stick it to the inside cover and end pages with spray adhesive.

5 Use craft glue to fix a small envelope to the center of the end page for your treasured items.

6 Make a cross on the inside cover for your keepsakes: Tie a knot in a length of raffia or ribbon. Thread through from the outside corner hole across the inside and out at the diagonal. Tie a knot on the outside and trim. Repeat on the opposite edge.

YOU WILL NEED

Spiral-bound notebook

Raffia

Tissue or fine paper *in contrasting colors*

Spray adhesive

Craft glue (PVA)

Small envelope

Ribbon

Piece of thin wood, *smaller than notebook*

Sand, shells, and starfish

Strong glue *(two-part epoxy)*

Pencil

Hole punch

Scissors

7 Spray adhesive over the piece of wood. Sprinkle over sand.

8 Form a collage with shells or other memorabilia and attach them using craft glue.

9 Mark out the position for the collage on the front cover of your notebook. Apply strong glue to the underside of the collage and press it firmly in place, taking care not to break fragile items.

10 Cut a length of ribbon long enough to tie around the book. Secure it with a knot around the central ring of the binding and tie it with a bow.

BELOW: *Inside the book covers, there are two handy places to keep loose items such as tickets, photos, shells, and postcards. Tuck larger ones inside the ribbon cross. Smaller ones can be stored in the envelope.*

Pocket-sized Travel Journal

A small-sized hard-cover journal like the one shown here is perfect for keeping a record of your travel or holiday memories. Again, make pockets to keep those special mementos.

YOU WILL NEED

2 pieces of book board, *4½ x 5½ in. (11 x 14 cm)*

2 sheets of handmade tea paper, *6½ x 7½ in. (16.5 x 19 cm)*

Wheat paste

Small brush

2 sheets of handmade tea paper, *4 x 5 in. (10 x 13 cm)*

Brayer *(small roller)*

Brick wrapped in paper, *as a weight*

35 sheets of letter-weight medium-brown paper, *5½ x 8½ in. (14 x 21 cm)*

Bone folder

Clip

2 pieces of ribbon, *1⅜ in. (3.5 cm) wide, 12 in. (30 cm) long*

Pencil

Bookbinder's needle

2 pieces of black waxed linen cord, *30 in. (75 cm) long*

Scissors

White glue

Piece of brown leather, *2¾ x 5½ in. (7 x 14 cm)*

Spatula

2 glassine envelopes, *3¾ x 4½ in. (9.5 x 11 cm)*

1 Using the hardcover techniques (see pages 43–45), cover each book board with 6½ x 7½ in. (16.5 x 19 cm) tea paper. Apply a sheet of 4 x 5 in. (10 x 13 cm) tea paper to the back of the book boards, and use the brayer to smooth the paper evenly. Place the book covers under a weight until they are dry; this should take at least 24 hours, depending upon humidity levels.

2 Prepare the text block by counting 35 sheets of medium-brown paper into seven stacks of five sheets each. Using a bone folder, fold each stack in half. Print lines on the pages or leave blank, as desired.

3 Place the sections in a stack and put under a weight for three to four hours. Remove the weight and secure at the head with a clip. Place a length of ribbon 1 in. (2.5 cm) from the tail of the stack, and with a pencil, mark on either side, running the pencil up and down the stack to mark each section. Repeat with a ribbon at the head of the book.

4 Remove the clip from the sections and pierce holes at each marking. Each section will have four holes, two on either side of where the ribbons will be placed.

5 Thread a bookbinder's needle with linen cord. Begin sewing in the first section by entering hole No. 3. Pull the needle and thread to the outside. Leave a tail of thread 5 in. (12.5 cm) long inside the section, and enter hole No. 4.

6 Place the ribbon in the loop of thread, and pull the thread taut to hold the ribbon in place.

7 Tie a double knot in the inside of the section.

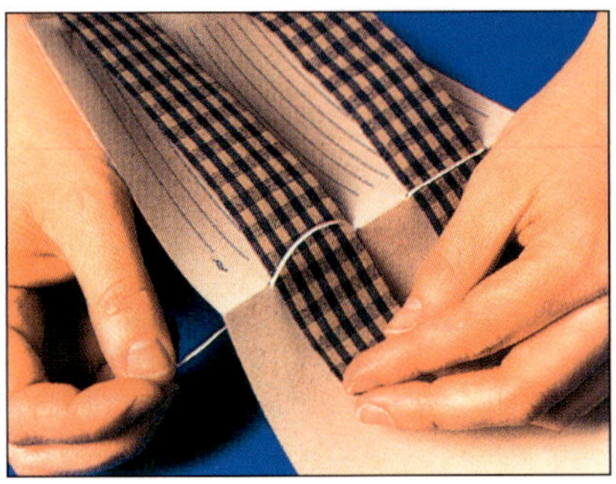

8 Enter hole No. 2 from the inside, then exit, and enter hole No. 1. Place the second ribbon within the loop and pull the thread taut.

9 Pull the thread through hole No. 2 to the outside of the section. Enter hole No. 2 of the next section and pull the thread to the inside. Enter hole No. 1, pulling the thread to the outside, and enter hole No. 2 again. Slip the ribbon into the loop of thread, and put this second section in place on the first section. Pull the thread taut and enter hole No. 3. Continue sewing in this manner until all sections have been added.

10 In the last section, tie a double knot on the inside of the section.

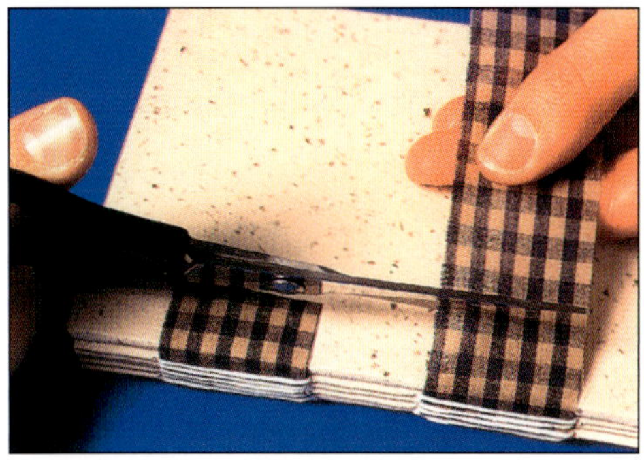

11 Trim the ribbons to 1½ in. (4 cm) on the front and back of the book.

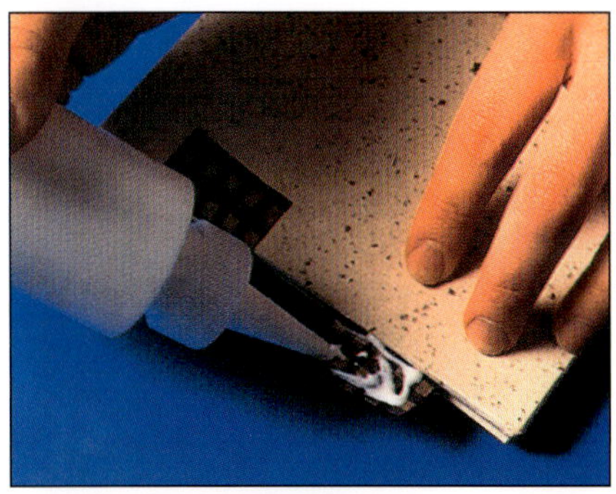

12 Apply a thin layer of white glue to the front of the ribbons. Be careful not to get glue on the pages.

13 Place a cover on top of the text block and smooth the ribbons in place. The line of the ribbons should be parallel to the head and tail of the book cover. Repeat with the back cover.

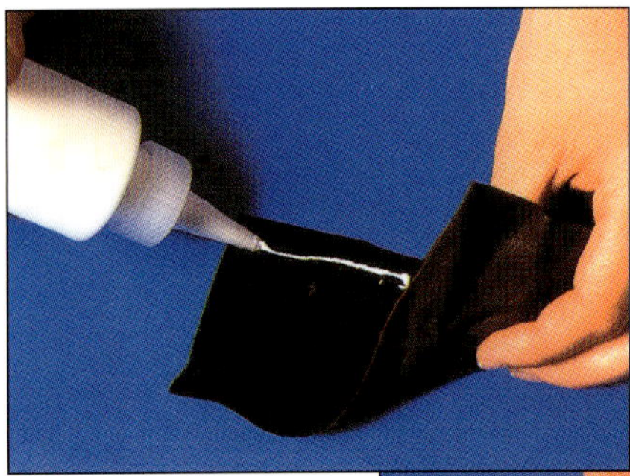

14 Apply a thin, even layer of white glue to the piece of leather.

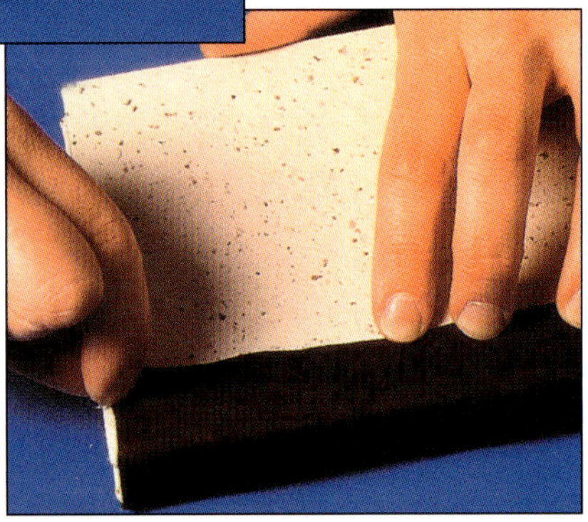

15 Position the leather on the spine of the book, tugging gently to wrap it evenly around the front and back of the book.

16 Apply a thin layer of white glue to the first page of the book.

17 Smooth the glue evenly over the page with a spatula.

18 Smooth the page down onto the cover using a brayer. This technique secures the cover to the text block. Repeat with the other cover.

19 Apply a thin layer of white glue to a glassine envelope.

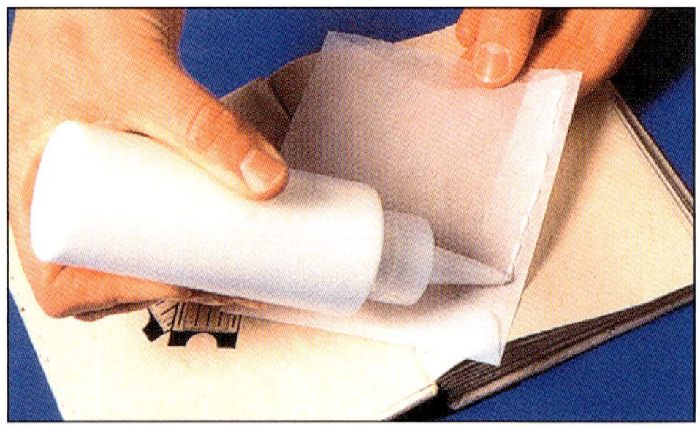

20 Position the envelope in the center of the inside front cover and smooth with a brayer. Repeat with a second glassine envelope on the inside back cover.

TIP: *Adhesive will seep through some parts of the ribbons. Gently wipe away excess glue and let dry. Most white glues will dry clear and matt.*

Travelog

No one seeing this box would suspect that it was anything other than a parcel, but it is really a clever way to store mementos collected on your travels. If you are too busy enjoying yourself to write a diary, ask your friends and family back home to save your postcards so that you can compile them on your return to bring back memories of faraway places.

Foreign stamps make good decorative material. Use them to line the video label that is visible through the plastic casing. Or for real authenticity, use bona fide stamps and mail it to yourself!

1 Remove the inner paper covers from the video boxes and replace them with a montage of travel mementos, such as stamps, ticket stubs, photographs, etc.

YOU WILL NEED

***2 plastic video boxes** (use the ones with no notch in the side edge)*

Travel mementos

Stamps

Brown paper

String

Sealing wax

2 Glue the video boxes together back to back, so that they both hinge open along the same edge.

3 Line the inside of the box with decorative paper and craft (PVA) glue. Cut a strip of brown paper approximately 4 x 18 in. (10 x 45 cm). Stick two-sided tape around the sides of the box excluding the spine, and attach the strip of brown paper.

4 Open up the video box and cut enough brown paper to form a parcel around the box. Snip the paper, as shown, and tuck the two excess ends back and fold over the ends as though you were wrapping a parcel.

Keep your travelog, postcards, letters, photographs, and keepsakes inside this cleverly designed parcel. Use one side for your journals and the other for postcards.

5 Close the boxes and stick on your collected travel stamps, if you have any. If not, you could buy some collectors' stamps.

6 Tie the boxes like a parcel with string and drip sealing wax onto the string at the back. Let the wax cool slightly before pressing a seal into it to leave an impression.

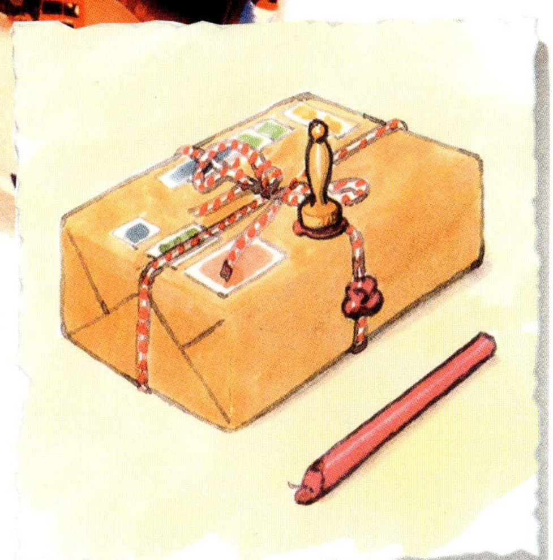

SCRAPBOOKS FOR ALL OCCASIONS

This chapter looks at making a selection of scrapbooks that can be used for all sorts of occasions. The following pages show an interesting colection of beautiful scrapbooks made from varied materials such as leaves and shells to feathers and flowers. In fact, anything you find could be used, its just a matter of putting things together in an aesthetic and creative way that's pleasing to you.

Victorian Scrapbook

This scrapbook is a celebration of Victorian design. The bookcloth is embossed with a floral pattern, the ribbon is extravagant, and the tiers of pockets are cut from sheets of hand-marbled papers.

1a Construct the scrapboards. Cut two pieces of binder's board to the desired height and width. My boards are 12 x 10½ in. (30 x 27 cm).

Cut decorative paper into eight strips:
Height = 4 in. (10 cm) (adjust this measurement to accommodate pockets of different depths)
Width = width of boards plus 2 in. (5 cm)

Cut bookcloth into six strips:
Height = 2½ in. (6 cm)
Width = width of boards plus 2 in. (5 cm)

Apply strips of pressure-sensitive adhesive to the right side of the bookcloth, along one long edge. Do not peel up the paper backing. Apply strips of pressure-sensitive adhesive to the wrong side of the decorative paper, along both long edges. Do not peel up paper backing. Apply a strip of pressure-sensitive adhesive to the entire width of the lower (tail) edge of each board. Do not peel up paper backing.

1b Adhere the decorative papers to the bookcloth strips. Peel off the backing paper from one edge of the decorative paper. Press the paper onto the cloth, approximately ⅛ in. (0.3 cm) away from the edge of the cloth without adhesive on it. Roll back the paper, peel off the backing strip from the cloth, and press the paper onto the cloth. Repeat with the other five strips. If your cloth tends to unravel, dip a finger into the PVA and run it along the exposed edge of cloth, sealing it.

Note: The pictures illustrating Step 2 are of small scale models of the actual scrapboards.

2a Assemble the scrapbooks. Place one of the two reserved decorative papers face down on the workbench. Remove the adhesive backing from the lower edge. Position the right side of the board (the side with the adhesive strip along its tail edge) on the paper, centered left to right and approximately 1 in. (2.5 cm) down from the head. Press.

2b Cut the corners, staying 1½ board thicknesses away from the tip of the board.

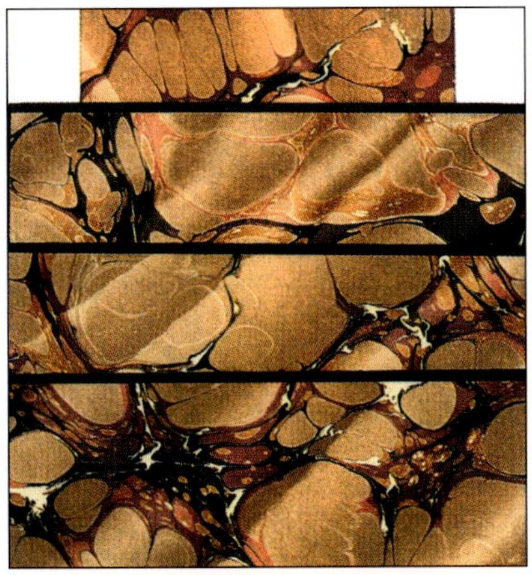

2c Apply adhesive to the two side (spine and fore-edge) turn-ins.

2d Bring the head turn-in onto the board and pinch in the corners.

2e Press the two side turn-ins onto the board.

2f To attach the first pocket, mark the board for its placement. Peel off the backing strip and stick down the pocket. Repeat with the second pocket. To adhere the third pocket, mark for its placement, remove the backing strip from the lower board edge, and stick down the pocket.

2g Turn the board over and complete the turn-ins. Starting with the upper pocket, apply strips of adhesive to the two side turn-ins; press them onto the board. Repeat with the second pocket. At the third pocket, first cut the corners and then bring in the long (tail) turn-ins before the two side ones.

2h-i Repeat Step 2 to complete the second scrapboard.

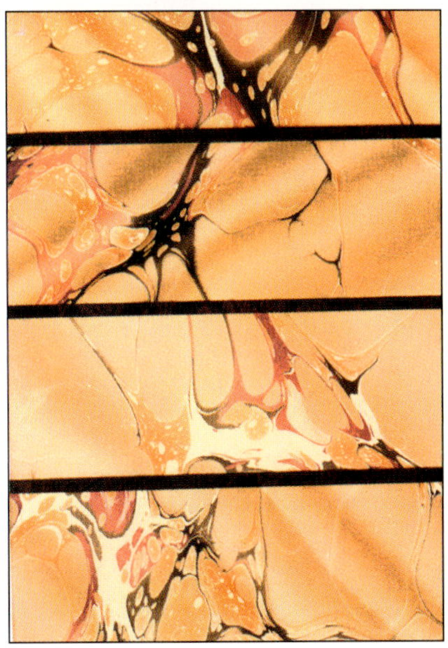

CUT OUT THE CASE UNITS:

The case is composed of three parts: Front and back, made of binder's board; and spine, cut from the flexible (bristol) board. There is no joint spacer. Pay attention to the grain direction that runs, as always, from head to tail.

CUT THE FRONT AND BACK CASE BOARD:
Height = height of scrapboards plus ¼ in. (0.5 cm)
Width = width of scrapboards plus ¼ in. (0.5 cm)

CUT THE SPINE PIECE:
Height = height of scrapboards plus ¼ in. (0.5 cm)
Width = thickness of the two scrapboards plus two (case) board thicknesses plus two cloth thicknesses, plus ⅛ in. (0.3 cm)

CUT THE BOOKCLOTH:
Height = height of case boards plus 1½ in. (4 cm)
Width = width of case boards, laid out, plus 1½ in. (4 cm)

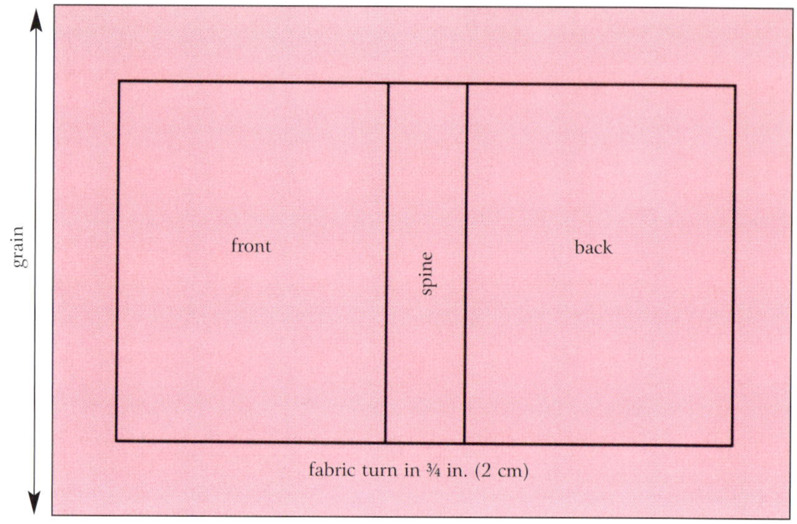

3 Construct the case by glueing out the boards and adhering them to the cloth (see drawing above). Cut the corners and complete the turn-ins.

Cut a hinge strip from the bookcloth:
Height = height of scrapboards,
Width = width of spine piece plus 2 in. (5 cm).

Apply mixture to the cloth, center it on the spine and press it firmly into place. Use your bone folder to sharply impress the edges of the case boards through the cloth.

Fill in the case. Cut two pieces of scrap paper large enough to fill in the area of exposed board on the inside of the case. Apply mixture to these papers and adhere them. This will counterbalance the pull of the boards toward the outside of the case. Put the finished case aside to dry, between newsprint sheets, under pressing boards and a weight.

4a Attach the ribbon ties. Make a pattern to determine the placement of the ties. Place the case, right side up, on a protected work surface. Transfer your placement mark to the case, and chisel. Repeat on the back board.

4b Push the ribbons, with the help of your micro-spatula, through the slits and glue them into place.

5 Finally, glue the scrapboards to the case. Apply undiluted PVA to the wrong side of a scrapboard. Remove excess glue from the edges. Center the board on the case board and press it into position. Hold it for a minute or two, until the glue begins to set. Put newsprint, a pressing board, and a weight on top. Repeat these steps to attach the second scrapboard, making sure the pockets on both boards are facing in the same direction. Leave the finished case under weights for several hours.

Natural Scrapbook

This book was made using a variety of handmade papers with just a hint of color to bring out the warmth of the natural materials. The ties are made from hemp cord knotted and embellished with a broken necklace from Thailand and a few wooden beads, while the clasp is made from a piece of driftwood found on a beach in Wales.

YOU WILL NEED

Grayboard

Paper for pages

Paper for guards

Endpapers

Cover paper

Cord, string, or waxed linen thread

A selection of beads

Driftwood or thin doweling

Matching sewing thread

Colored thread for attaching ties

PVA glue

Wheatflour paste

Waxed paper for pressing

A scrapbook can contain papers of considerable thickness, as long as it has corresponding guards at the spine to accommodate the extra bulk and stop the book becoming wedge-shaped. The guards in this particular book are made from Indian silk paper and scraps of the cover paper. The guards are torn instead of cut, which gives them a softer appearance more in keeping with the feel of the book.

1 Fold the paper for the pages. Tear the guards to size and place a guard (or two if the papers are very thin) between each fold of paper. Assemble into sections.

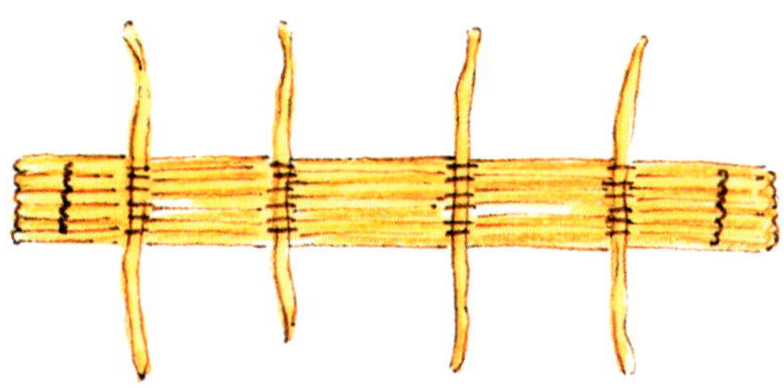

2 Sew the sections to cords or thongs, using matching sewing thread.

3 Cut two boards ⅛ in. (3mm) larger than the papers at the head, foot, and fore-edge. Mark the boards for lacing in the cords and cut recesses on the front and back of the board. Cover the boards, cutting and glueing corners and turn-ins.

4 Lace on your covered boards.

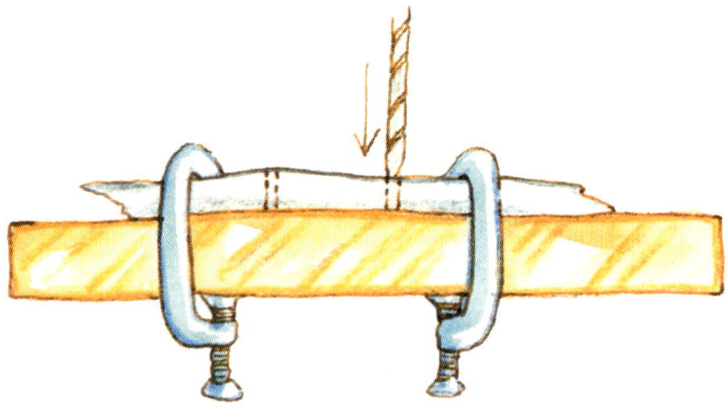

5 Make the clasp by drilling two holes through the driftwood or doweling with a small drill. You will need to clamp the wood down to hold it in position and remember to use plenty of spare boards to protect your work surface.

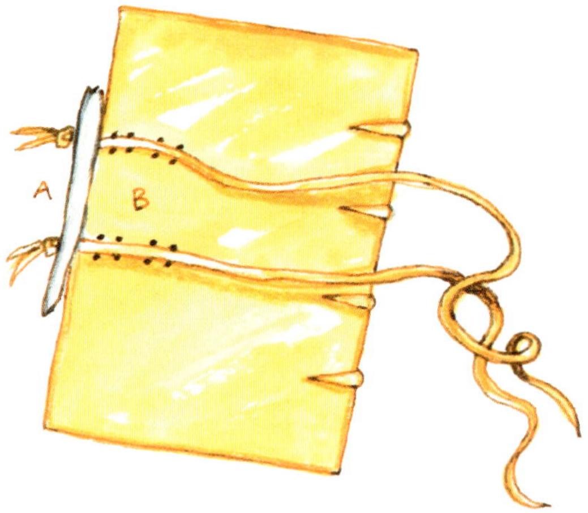

6 Make two ties, five times the width of the book, from twine, cord, threads, or string and tie one at each end of the clasp (A). Then take the two ties to the book cover board and mark sewing positions (B).

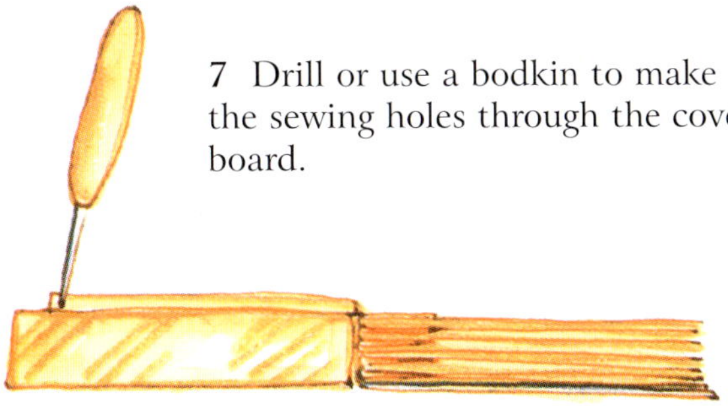

7 Drill or use a bodkin to make the sewing holes through the cover board.

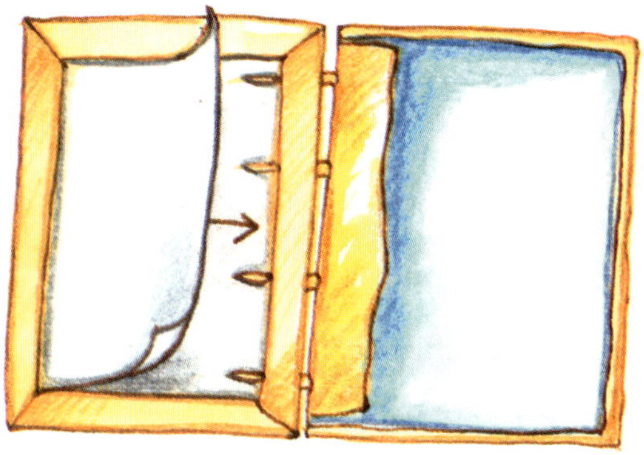

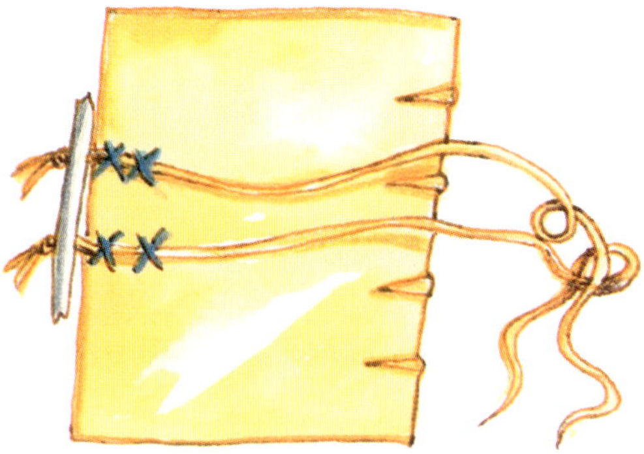

8 Attach the ties with stitching of your choice, using colored thread. You may need to sew through, as well as over, the ties since they may slide around.

9 Wrap the ties around the book, knotting and heading the cords as you go. When you are happy with how the ties look, unwrap them.

10 The next step is filling-in, that is optional and can be applied to many projects in this book. Filling-in gives a stylish finish to the insides of the boards and allows you to remove lumps and bumps caused by lacing-in and sewing.

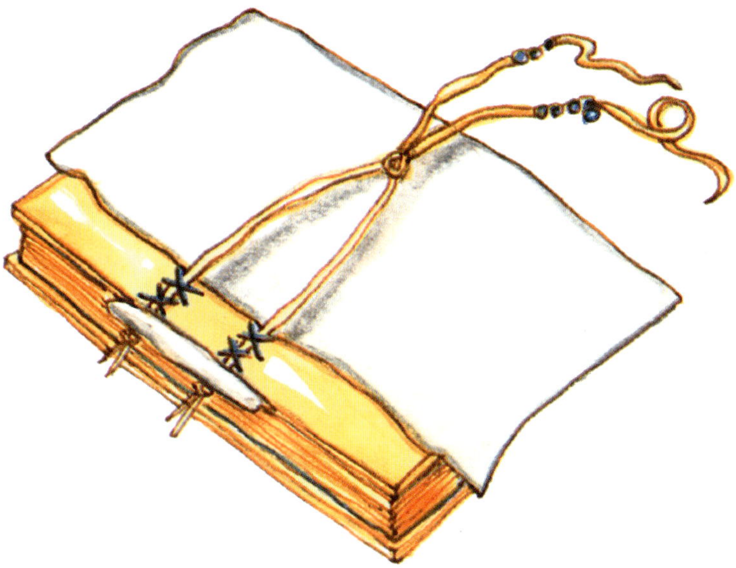

11 Cut the endpapers the same size as the pages of the book. Paste them down with wheatflour paste and put a sheet of waxed or blotting paper between them. Then put a piece of thick, protective paper (with a torn edge) under the ties on the back board to avoid any unwanted impressions. Put the book under a weight between waxed paper and pressing boards to dry overnight. When the endpapers are dry, the book can be tied and the cord wrapped around the wooden clasp.

Window Scrapbook

A window on the front cover may be used to hold a favorite photo or drawing to set the theme for your memory album. The use of spacers will allow you to add photographs, clippings, and special memories to the pages in this scrapbook.

You can add final touches to your scrapbook cover with colorful handmade paper and mementos of holidays gone by.

YOU WILL NEED

Wheat paste

Small brush

2 sheets of handmade moss and petals paper, *14 x 17 in. (35 x 43 cm)*

2 pieces of book board, *12 x 12 in. (30 x 30 cm)*

2 sheets of yellow machine-made paper, *10 x 11¼ in. (25 x 28 cm)*

White glue

Brayer

Brick wrapped in paper as a weight

10 sheets of white machine-made paper, *11¾ x 13½ in. (29.5 x 33 cm)*

Ruler

Pencil

Bone folder

2 clamps

Sheet of paper *for template for binding holes*

Hammer

Awl

Bookbinder's needle

Piece of tan leather cord, 40 in. *(110 cm) long*

Craft knife

Steel ruler

Cutting mat

Sheet of handmade moss and petals paper, *8½ x 11 in. (21 x 28 cm)*

1 Paste a sheet of 14 x 17 in. (35 x 43 cm) moss and petals paper to the back cover book board. Repeat with the front cover book board, taking special care to miter the corners.

2 Apply a sheet of yellow machine-made paper to the inside of each cover using white glue. Roll in place using a brayer. Place both covers under a weight for 24 to 48 hours or until dry.

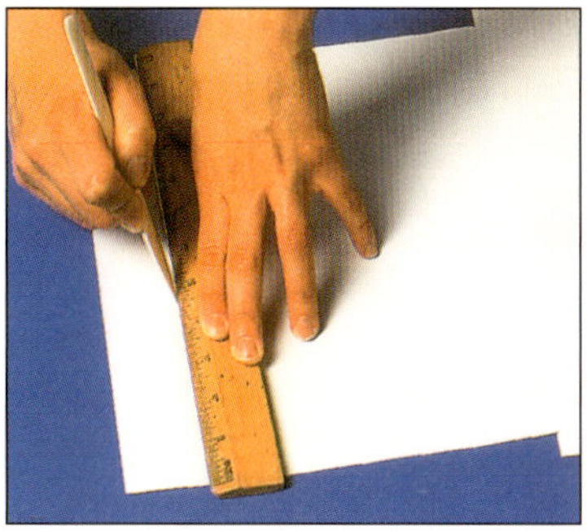

3 Create a spacer between each inner page by folding a 1½ in. (3.5 cm) flap on each sheet. Use a ruler and pencil to mark 1½ in. (3.5 cm) from the edge, and make a crease with a bone folder. The folded page should now measure 11¾ x 11¾ in. (29.5 x 29.5 cm).

4 Repeat with each page.

TIP: *It is often a good idea to add spacers to a scrapbook when it will be filled with bulky materials. The added space between each sheet reduces bulging by making room for added thickness.*

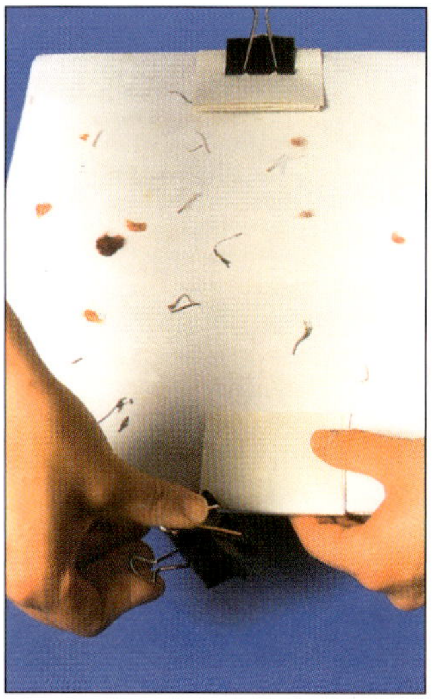

5 To assemble the book covers and pages, first place the back cover down, with the yellow paper side facing upward. Place the stack of book pages on the back cover, each with the flap on the left side, folded face up. Finally, place the front cover on top of the stack, with the moss and petals side facing upward, and with the hinge on the left-hand side. Secure the book with a clamp at both the head and tail of the book.

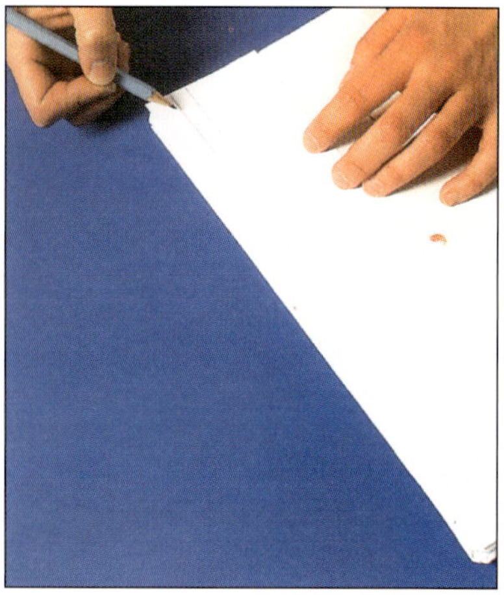

6 Create a paper template for binding holes by marking the following: a) four holes 1 in. (2.5 cm) from the spine and 1 in. (2.5 cm) from the head and tail, with 3¼ in. (8 cm) between each hole; and b) three holes ¾ in. (2 cm) from the head and tail, with 3¼ in. (8 cm) between each hole.

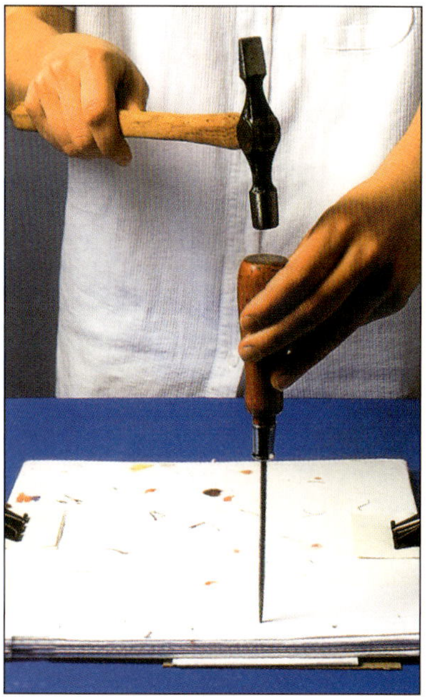

7 Using a hammer and awl, pierce the holes through the covers and text block.

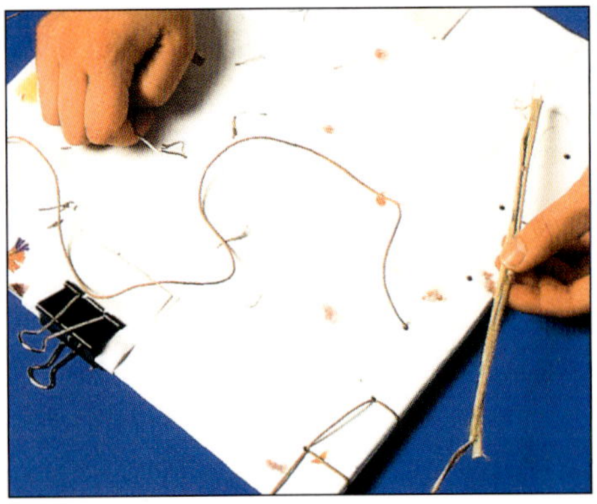

8 Thread a bookbinder's needle with leather cord. Begin sewing at the back of the book. At the third hole from the top, place the twig in place and sew over it to secure in place.

9 Continue sewing down the spine of the book. Sew to the top of the book and tie the cords off when you reach the top hole.

10 To create a frame for the cover of the book, cut a rectangle measuring 4½ x 5½ in. (11 x 14 cm) from the center of the cardboard. Work on a cutting mat to protect the work surface. The remaining frame should measure 5½ x 7 in. (14 x 18 cm) with the top and bottom sides of the frame ¾ in. (2 cm) wide and the left and right sides of the frame 1 in. (2.5 cm) wide. Apply wheat paste to the frame and place it on a (8½ x 11 in. (21 x 28 cm) sheet of handmade moss and petal paper.

11 Turn the frame over and use a brayer to smooth it.

12 Using a steel ruler and craft knife, cut two diagonal slits, creating four triangles of paper in the center of the frame.

13 Fold the paper outward over the frame and fix in place using wheat paste.

14 Trim the excess paper leaving a 1 in. (2.5 cm) flap along each side.

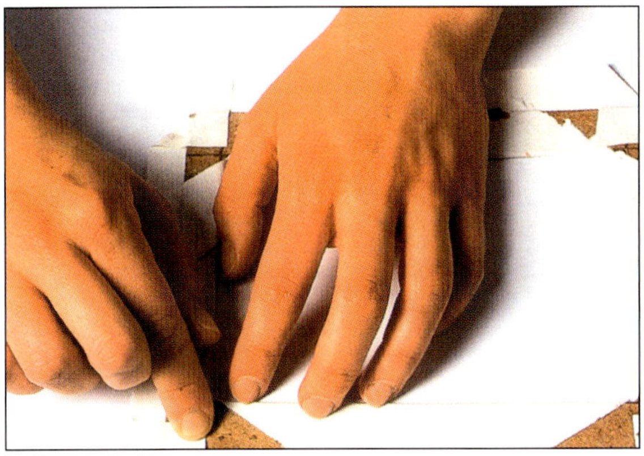

15 Miter the corners and paste in place.

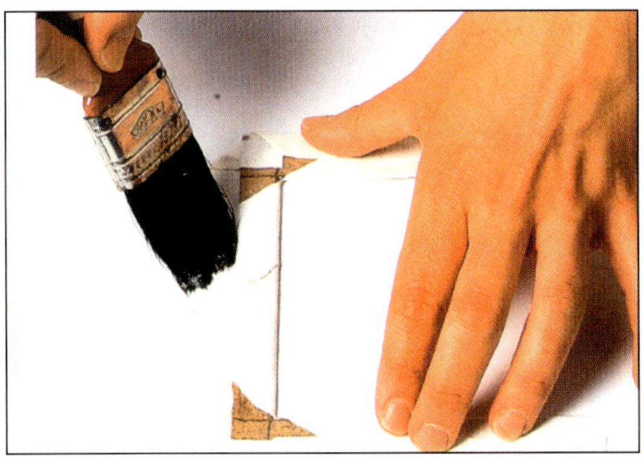

16 Paste the edges and smooth in place.

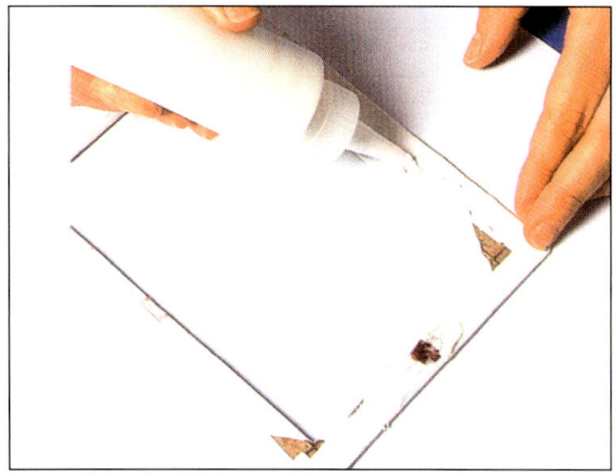

17 Apply a thin layer of white glue to the bottom, left and right edges of the frame. Leave the top edge unglued to allow a picture to be slipped into the frame.

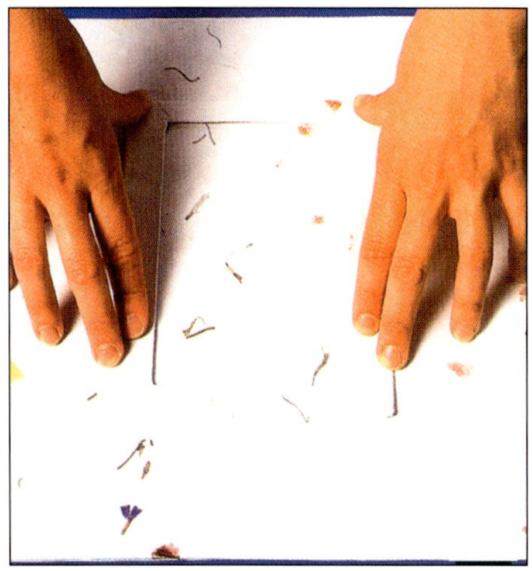

18 Place the frame, glue side down, centered on the cover of the book and positioned with the unglued edge at the head of the book.

Every piece of handmade paper is unique and the examples shown here have been made using an assortment of different petals and leaves.

Window Scrapbook (2)

This is another variation of a window scrapbook and the cut-out panel on the front board allows you to create a combined cover design and first title page. The small image used on the front of this book is a lino cut made using water-based printing ink and hand-painted with watercolors. The image is mounted on a piece of Mexican bark paper that forms a visual link between the color of the pages and the cover paper. The binding is elegant and easy to make using eyelets and a silk cord.

YOU WILL NEED

Grayboard
Cover paper
Eyelets
Paper for pages
Lining paper
Waxed paper for pressing
Cord for binding
Print, drawing, photograph, etc. for front cover
Masking tape
PVA glue and wheatflour paste
Knife/scalpel
Cutting mat or board
Steel ruler
Bone folder
Dividers
Glue and paste brushes
Eyelet punch
Pressing boards

1 Cut and fold paper for the pages to size. This model has four sections of four pages, but you can use as many as you like. With dividers, mark in ¾ in. (2 cm) from the folded edge of each section, and, using a bone folder and ruler, score and crease along these points (A).

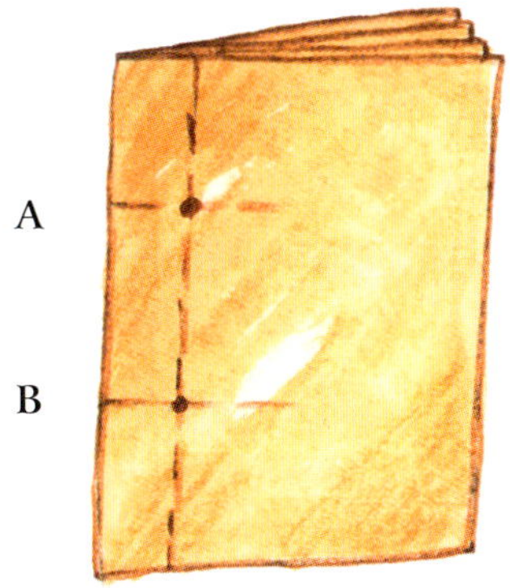

2 Measure the height of the book and divide into three. Punch or drill holes at the two points (A and B) through each section.

3 Cut two cover boards ⅛ in. (3 mm) larger than the book all round. Using one section as a pattern, transfer the position of the holes to both boards and punch them out.

4 Measure ¾ in. (2 cm) from the spine edge of the board (where you have just punched the holes) and cut this strip away. Repeat with the other board, then put the spine strips to one side.

5 Trim away ¼ in. (5 mm) from the edge of the two larger pieces of board (A) to produce the joint allowance.

6 Mount your image on a piece of decorative paper and trim to size; in this example it is 1¾ x 2 in. (4.5 x 5 cm).

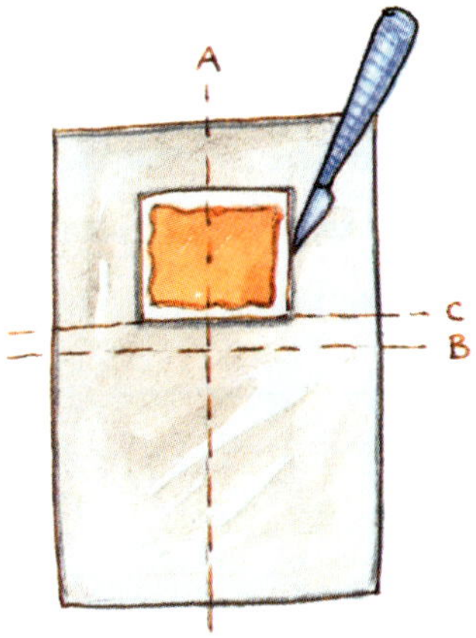

7 To cut the window in the front board, find the center point by dividing the board in half lengthwise and widthwise (A and B). Measure ½ in. (1 cm) up from the center line (C), position your artwork and add ¼ in. (5 mm) to each edge. Cut out the area inside this border.

8 Cut two strips of bookcloth, 1¼ in. (3 cm) wide and the height of the boards, and attach one edge of each strip to each of the spine strips with glue.

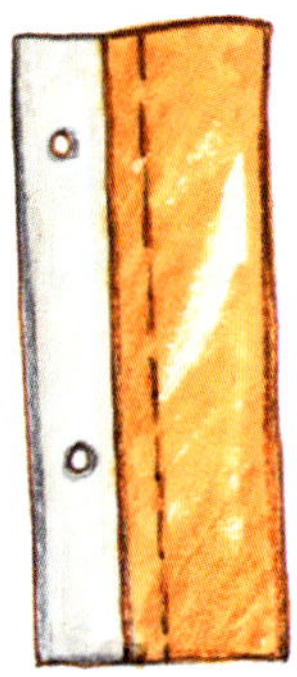

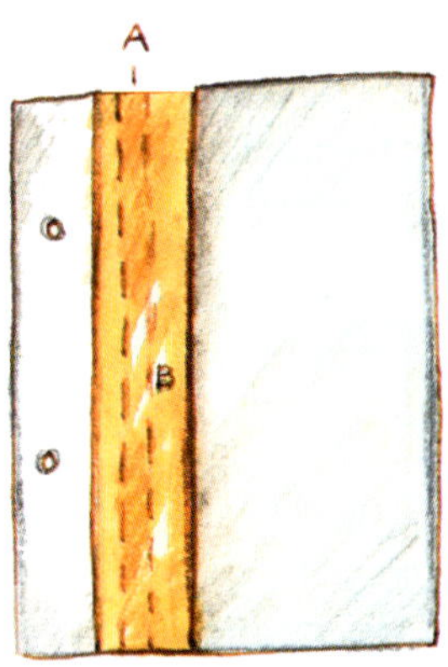

9 Mark two points on the cloth ¼ in. (5 mm) away from the edge of the spine piece (A). Coat the inside edge of the cover board with glue and attach to the cloth (B).

10 Cut four tiny strips of cover paper ⅛ x ⅜ in. (3 x 8 mm) and glue them around the inner corners of the window on the front board.

11 Cut two pieces of cover paper approximately ⅘ in. (2 cm) larger than the boards on all four sides. Coat the boards with glue and apply the paper, rubbing down well into the joints through a piece of clean paper. Trim the turn-ins to ⅝ in. (1.5 cm), fold and cut the corners as usual and glue down the turn-ins. Leave the boards to dry under a weight between clean or waxed paper and pressing boards.

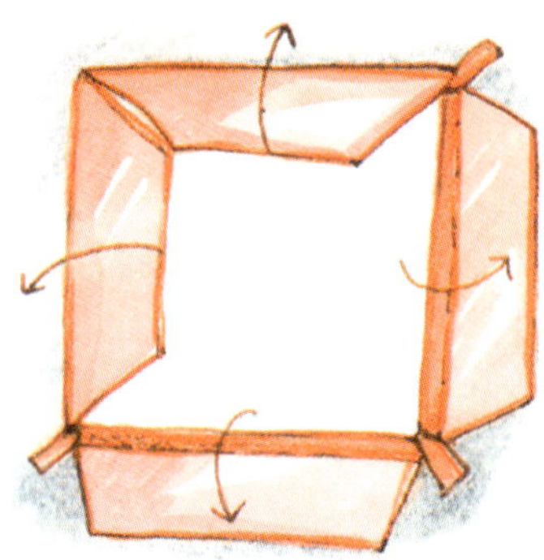

12 To turn the cover paper at the window, trim the paper as illustrated, cutting diagonally into each corner. Trim the turn-ins to ⅝ in. (1.5 cm) and glue down. Using a bone folder, carefully work the paper into the corners of the window. When the glue is dry, trim the turn-ins on the inside of the boards back to ⅛ in (3 mm) for neatness.

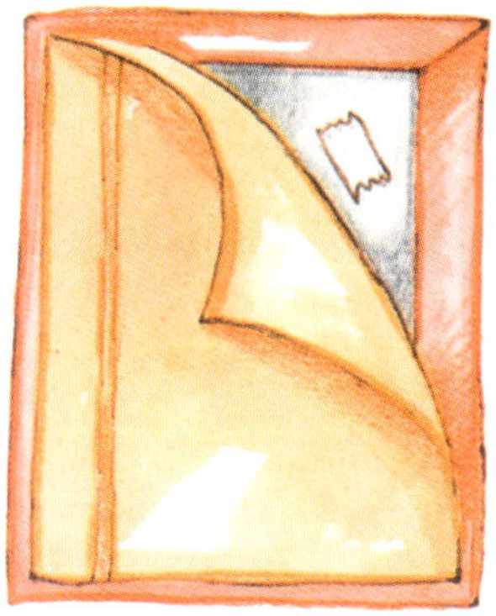

13 Cut two pieces of lining paper ⅛ in. (3 mm) smaller than the boards on all four edges. Place one of the linings in position on the front board and anchor it temporarily with masking tape. Turn the board over and transfer the size of the cut-out to the lining paper by scoring around the edge of the window with a bone folder. Remove the paper from the board and peel off the masking tape.

14 Cut out the square from the lining paper, taking away an extra 1/16 in. (1 mm) to allow for the thickness of the cover paper. Coat the lining papers with wheatflour paste, position them on the boards and rub down. Press, then leave under a weight between waxed or blotting paper and pressing boards to dry.

15 Cut through the paper covering the punched holes and work the excess into the recesses, then press in the eyelets using an eyelet punch.

16 Paste your artwork in position on the front page of your book and leave to dry under a weight between waxed paper and pressing boards.

17 To finish your journal, take the cord through the eyelets as illustrated in the diagram, knotting both ends to prevent them from fraying.

Mosaic Scrapbook

For this project you will need to keep any beautiful sweet wrappers because when they are smoothed out they make exquisite decorations. Here, a recess has been cut, in which the foils are laid. Several layers of waterproof varnish protect the foils and give them a jewel-like quality. The endpapers have been decorated with inks and snippets of confetti-like foil to complement the cover.

1 Decide how much of your book you want to decorate and rough out your design on paper. Mark out the area on the book to be used. Using a scalpel, score a recess 1/16 in. (1 mm) into the cover along your markings.

YOU WILL NEED

Artist's drawing book

Colored sweet wrappers

Double-sided tape

Water-soluble varnish

Colored elastic cord

4 sequins

Inks and pencil

Ruler

Scalpel

Scissors

Paintbrushes

2 Using the tip of your scalpel, ease out the first corner. You should then be able to pull off this layer.

3 Smooth out your foil wrappers, using your finger or a flat implement. Stick double-sided tape to the wrong side of each piece you intend to use.

5 Stick the foils into the recess. Either layer your background colors first, then add other pieces, or fit the shapes together like a jigsaw.

4 Cut your planned shapes out of the foil wrappers and remove the tape backing as required.

6 Apply several coats of water-soluble varnish (solvent-based varnish may take the color off the foil). Leave each coat to dry before applying the next.

7 Stick down colored elastic cord the width of your recess. Glue a sequin onto each corner.

8 Paint the endpapers with inks. Choose colors that fit your scheme. If you want a really rich color, apply several layers of ink, letting each coat dry between applications.

9 Snip more foil to decorate the endpages. Remove the tape backing and position as desired.

10 Apply varnish to the decorated endpages to protect them.

Sweet wrappers make fabulous decorating materials as they come in such sumptuous colors. Create a design with them to decorate the front of your book.

VARIATION

To create a rose-petal window, cut a rectangle right through the cover with a scalpel. Cut two pieces of acetate ½ in. (1 cm) larger than the window. Sandwich handmade paper rose petals between the sheets and stick the acetate together with craft glue. Stick this to the inside front cover and hide the window edge with gold thread.

Treasured Possessions

This book is designed for those who love to collect bits and pieces that are generally put in a box, in the bottom of a drawer, and then forgotten. There is even a coin collector's drawer to hold bulky or delicate items, and the fabric pages can be used to stitch favorite fragments of ribbon, fabric, or embroidery to keep them safe.

YOU WILL NEED

Foam board (polyboard)

Assorted ribbons

Fabric for cover

Ring binder

Fusible webbing

Coin collector's drawer with compartment tray

Clear, plastic/acetate sheets

1 Cut a piece of foam board and a piece of webbing, each 11 x 14 in. (28 x 35 cm). The board is there as a support. Cut the ribbons 13¾ in. (34 cm) long and pin them along the top and bottom through the webbing and into the foam board to form a warp.

2 Cut weft ribbons 10¾ in. (27 cm) long and weave them over and under the warp ribbons until the board is covered. Pin the weft ribbons at each end. Cover the woven ribbons with a clean pressing cloth and press with a hot iron to fuse the ribbons to the webbing. Remove the woven ribbons from the foam board, and press the weft ribbons again on the reverse side.

The cover is made of woven ribbons. Practice this technique before making the cover itself and play with the colors to achieve a pleasing combination.

3 Cut the front and back cover fabric as one piece measuring 16 x 27½ in. (40 x 67 cm). Place the ribbonwork panel on the right side of the cover fabric, as shown, allowing a 1¼-in. (3-cm) border around the sides. Attach ribbonwork panel with fusible webbing, using an iron on the reverse side of the cover fabric.

4 Using small stitches, attach a border of ribbon. Add any embellishments as desired—here, large mother-of-pearl buttons were used.

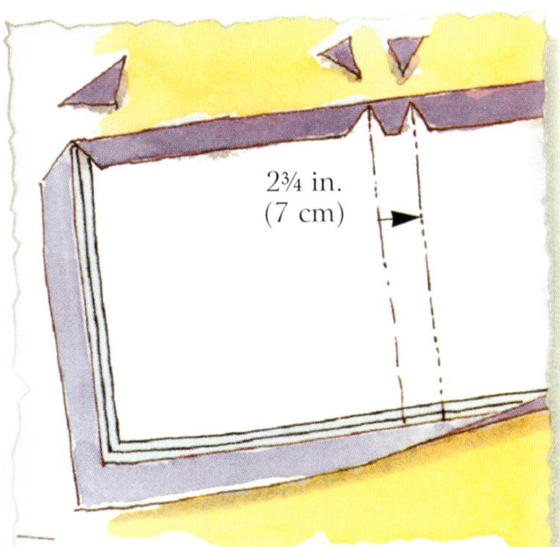

5 Cut out a piece of foam board (polyboard) 14 x 24 in. (35 x 60 cm). Cut partway through two parallel lines 2¾ in. (7 cm) apart to make the spine in the center of the book. On the uncut side of the foam board, make a border of two-sided tape. Place the cut side of the board on the wrong side of the cover fabric. Make sure the ribbonwork panel is in the right position, then fold over the edges of the fabric, and attach them carefully and smoothly to the tape. Be sure to allow for the book to open and close.

6 Cut a piece of fabric 14½ x 24½ in. (36 x 62 cm) for the inside cover. Iron under a ½-in. (1-cm) hem all around and place it on the covered board so that it sticks to the remaining tape. Slipstitch round the edges to finish the cover.

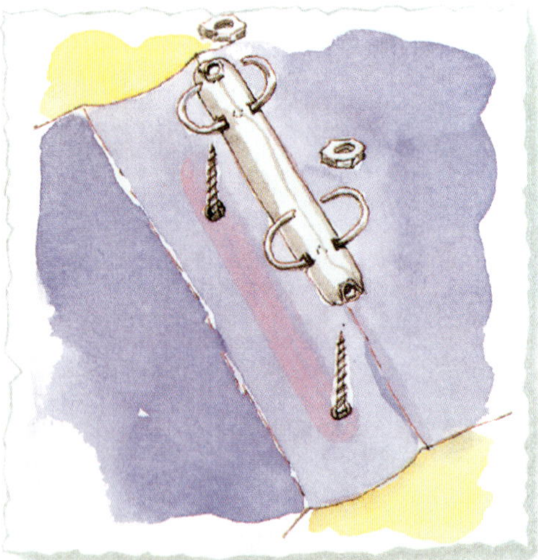

7 Place a ring clasp in the correct position along the inside spine and pierce holes to correspond through the foam board. Attach the clasp, using small nuts and bolts.

8 Cut a strip of foam board 1 x 34 in. (2.5 x 85 cm). Measure 12 in. (30 cm) from each end and cut through partway, then fold the strip into a U shape, as shown. Glue this into position on the inside back cover. Weigh down with a book while drying.

9 Glue the plastic cover of the collector's drawer into the U shape along its sides. Glue ¾-in. (2-cm) velvet ribbon around the sides of the drawer holder and ½-in. (1-cm) ribbon along the top edges to cover and finish the joins.

10 To make pages, cut pieces of sturdy fabric (linen was used here) approximately 13 x 14 in. (32 x 34 cm) and iron a piece of webbing the same size onto each one. Using pinking shears, cut the backed fabric to measure 12 x 13 in. (30 x 32 cm). Cut one strip of thin cardboard 1 x 12 in. (2.5 x 30 cm) for each page. Fold the fabric over to the wrong (backed) side, insert a strip of cardboard, and iron it in place, as shown. Use a hole punch to make holes and place the pages in the binder.

11 You could choose to cover the album clasp if you like, although it was left uncovered for the finished project here. To cover the clasp, cut a piece of fabric, or a broad strip of velvet ribbon, large enough to cover the ring clasp. Cut two slits for the clasps and stitch into place.

TIP: *If you cannot buy a ring-binder clasp, cut one out of an old folder and glue it onto the spine.*

Scallop Shell Scrapbook

Flat scallop shells form a witty little scrapbook to write down poems, impressions, special thoughts, or those special items you wish to keep. The pages have been roughly torn out of mottled paper to add to the organic nature of the book and the elastic binding allows it to open flat. To finish, the shells were burnished with metallic wax, adding that special touch.

Roughly torn pages are sandwiched between two flat scallop shells to make a clever and organic little scrapbook.

1 Use a pencil to mark two evenly placed slots on the flat end of each scallop. Secure the scallops with putty. Clamp and drill the holes in the marked points.

2 Draw round one of the shells onto the mottled paper and mark out the holes.

3 Tear out the shell shapes so that you have rough edges. You will need about 50 shell-shaped sheets for the book.

4 Make holes with a hole punch using a size to suit your binding elastic or ribbon—possibly a ⅛ in. (3 mm) punch.

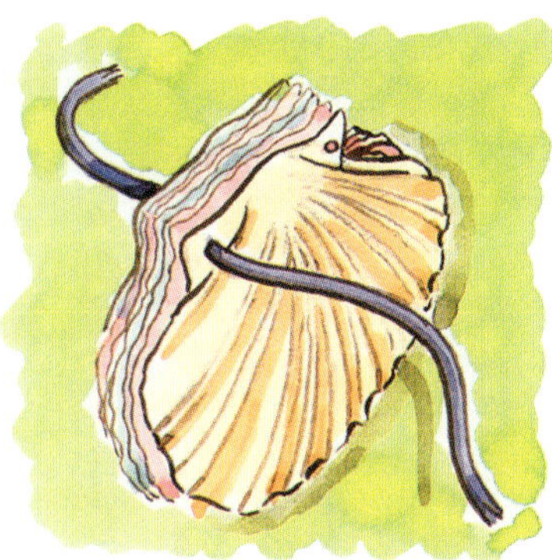

5 Thread the elastic or ribbon from the bottom shell through all the pages and the top cover shell.

6 Cross the elastic or ribbon over the spine of the book, then insert it through the second set of holes.

7 Tie the two remaining ends into a knot around the diagonal elastic, forming a cross. Make sure this is secure before trimming off the ends.

YOU WILL NEED

2 small-size flat scallop shells *(available from craft suppliers or seafood stores)*

Mottled or speckled paper in seashore hues

Round elastic or ribbon

Gold/silver metallic wax and soft cloth

Putty (Blu-Tak)

Clamp

Drill and fine bit

Hole punch

Scissors

Each scallop shell is unique with its own special markings—that's what makes them a perfect choice, for a one-of-a-kind natural notebook.

8 Using a soft cloth, buff the scallop shells with gold or silver metallic wax.

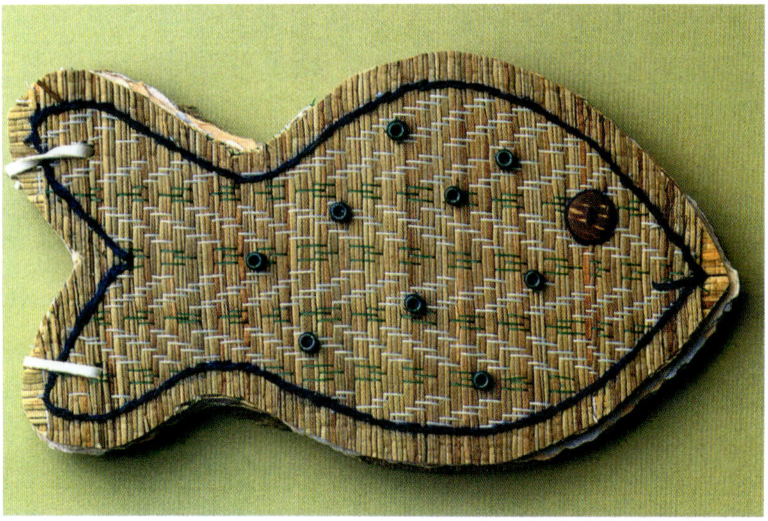

VARIATION

Use an old straw beach mat and speckled paper to make an organic fish-shaped notebook to jot down your beach impressions.

1 Using a fish template, cut eight identical fish shapes from the beach mat. Layer four of the fish on top of each other and sew around the fish shape with strong wool in back stitch ½ in. (1 cm) from the edge. Repeat for the back cover. Cut fish-shaped paper.

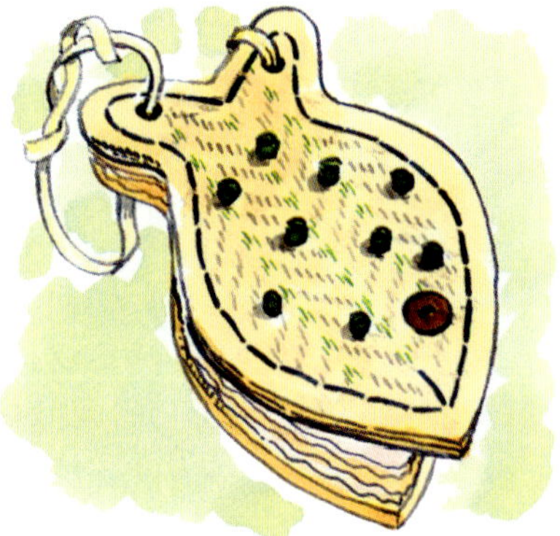

2 Make two small holes in the tails of each fish with the point of a sharp knife. Sew on a button for the eye of the fish and sew beads on at random. Insert pages between the covers. Thread elastic through the covers and pages and tie securely.

Post and Screw

This book is both beautiful and practical. Pages may easily be added or removed because of the post and screw binding. The raffia tie closure is an attractive design feature and complements the grass paper used for the cover.

The raffia tie complements the handmade paper beautifully.

YOU WILL NEED

Sheet of book board, 5½ x 7½ in. (14 x 19 cm)

Sheet of book board, 5½ x 6 in. (14 x 15 cm)

2 sheets of handmade prairie grass paper, 8½ x 11 in. (21 x 28 cm)

Wheat paste

Small brush

White glue

2 lengths of raffia

2 sheets of handmade prairie grass paper, 5 x 7 in. (12.5 x 18 cm)

Brick wrapped in paper, as a weight

2 sheets of white medium-weight vellum

15 sheets of handmade classic cotton paper, 5 x 7 in. (12.5 x 18 cm)

Sheet of book board, 1 x 5½ in. (2.5 x 14 cm), for template

Hammer

Awl

2 posts and screws

Screwdriver

1 Paste and cover the front and back boards with handmade prairie grass paper.

2 Cut or tear a small piece of prairie grass paper to approximately 2 x 3 in. (5 x 7.5 cm). Apply a layer of white glue over the paper. Position a strip of raffia at the fore-edge of the book, and cover the end with pasted prairie grass paper. Repeat with the back cover.

3 Paste and apply a sheet of 5 x 7 in. (12.5 x 18 cm) prairie grass paper to the inside of the front cover. Repeat with the back cover. Place the cover under a weight to dry.

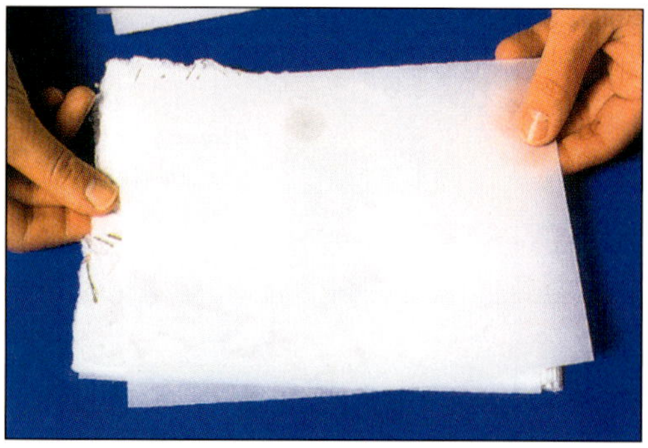

4 Cut two sheets of vellum measuring 5 x 7 in. (12.5 x 18 cm).

5 Place a sheet of vellum on either side of the stack of classic cotton paper. Place the stack between the book covers and secure with clips.

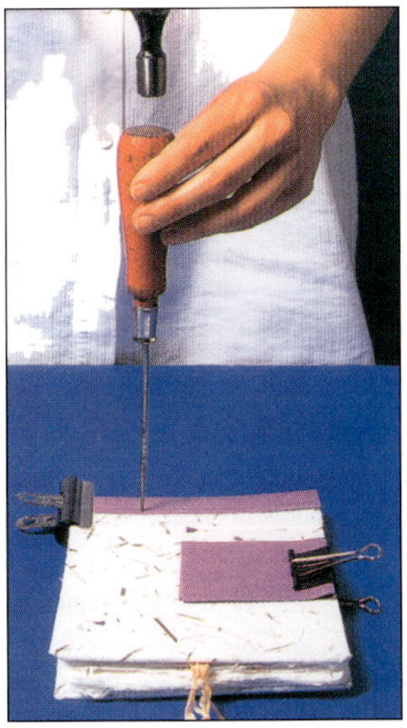

6 Create a template for the two holes ¾ in. (2 cm) in from the edge of the spine and 1½ in. (4 cm) from the head and tail. Attach the template to the book spine and pierce the holes using a hammer and awl.

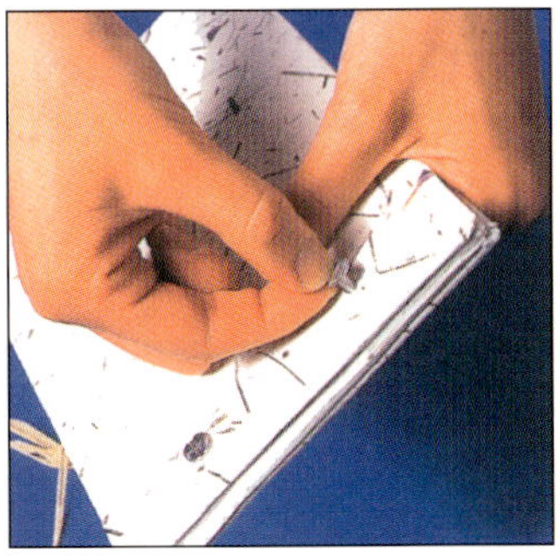

7 Insert the post and screw into each hole. Tighten with a screwdriver.

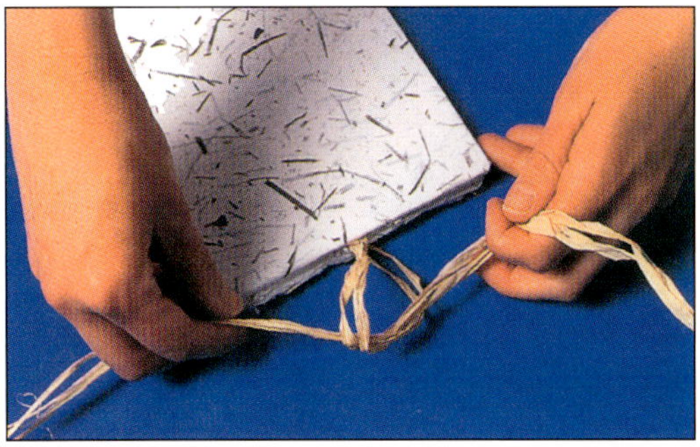

8 Tie a bow on the fore-edge with raffia ties.

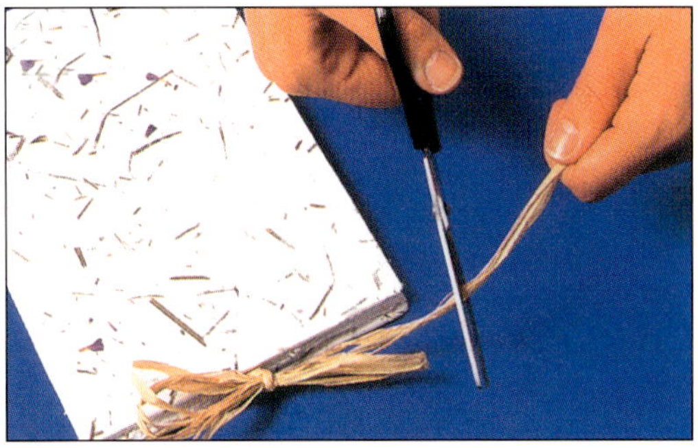

9 Trim the ends to make the bow neater.

The post and screw mechanism is usually available in copper or silver tones and in a variety of sizes. When making the holes, select a drill bit or awl that is slightly smaller than the post and screw. This will create a hole that remains tight once the post is inserted.

Simple Scrapbook

This simple idea combines a scrapbook with a collector's album. Colorful sheets of construction paper can be used for photographs and writings, while transparent coin-display pages allow you to include small precious mementos without needing to glue them down. For larger keepsakes, such as postcards and party invitations, you can add transparent photograph album sleeves.

YOU WILL NEED

Matt board (mounting card)
Plastic coin-display pages
Cutting mat
Hole punch
Construction paper or fabric
Lightweight cardboard

1 Cut a piece of matt board (mounting card) slightly larger than the transparent paper pages you are using. Cut two lines partway through for the spine. Take a piece of lightweight cardboard and cut it at least ½ in. (1 cm) smaller around all edges.

2 Glue the matt board to the covering paper or fabric, using craft glue. Allow enough give for the cover to open and close by working the fabric or covering paper into the scored lines.

3 Take the lightweight cardboard cut in Step 1 and glue it to the inside of the cover.

This flexible format gives you the freedom to arrange and reorganize your mementos easily, creating a living, dynamic personal museum.

Using plastic coin-collector album pages allows you to see both sides of small items such as ticket stubs.

4 Intersperse each transparent page with a piece of lightweight cardboard of the same size. Punch holes in the cardboard pages to match those on the plastic pages.

5 You can use differently colored lightweight cardboard interspersed between the transparent photograph sleeves for variety.

6 Add sheets of blank or decorative paper for the scrapbook section, marking holes as in Step 4.

7 Line up the decorative pages, photographic sleeves, and transparent pages and punch holes in the back cover to match those on the pages. Thread ribbon up through the back cover and pages and tie in a bow.

Single-section Scrapbook

For someone new to making scrapbooks, this project is a good place to start. The single section makes a fine little book as it is, or it may be given added covering and decorative touches.

YOU WILL NEED

8 sheets of cotton and petals handmade paper, *8½ x 11 in. (21 x 28 cm)*

Bone folder

Medium-weight white vellum, *8½ x 11 in. (21 x 28 cm)*

Craft knife

Steel ruler

Cutting mat

Medium-weight sage paper, *9 x 12 in. (23 x 30 cm)*

Pencil and clips

Awl and hammer

3 strands of green embroidery thread, *18 in. (45 cm) long*

Bookbinder's needle

Scissors

Sheet of rust paper *cut to 4½ x 7 in. (11 x 18 cm)*

White glue

Preserved leaf

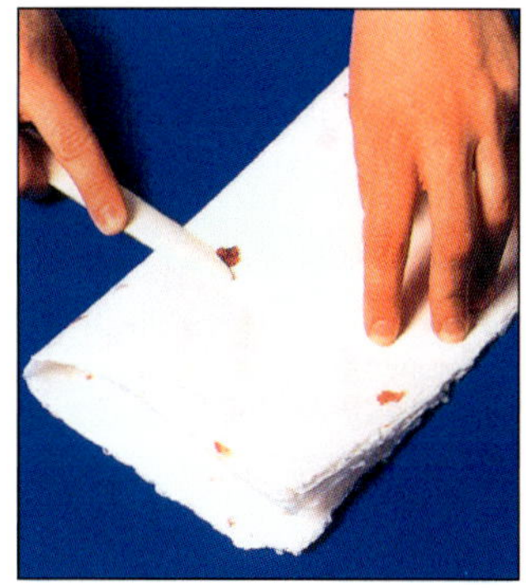

1 Select eight sheets of 8½ x 11 in. (21 x 28 cm) cotton and petals paper. Jog the stack together. Fold the stack in half using a bone folder.

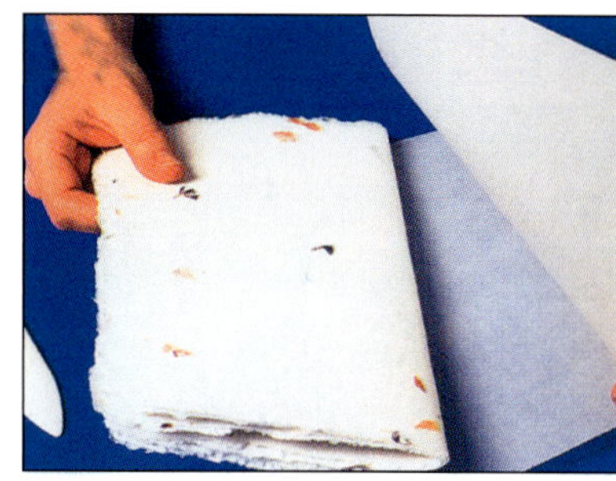

2 Create a flyleaf by folding one sheet of 8½ x 11 in. (21 x 28 cm) vellum in half. Slip the cotton and petals section into the flyleaf to prepare for binding.

3 Using a craft knife and steel ruler, and working on a cutting mat to protect the work surface, cut a cover of medium-weight sage paper, measuring 9 x 12 in. (23 x 30 cm).

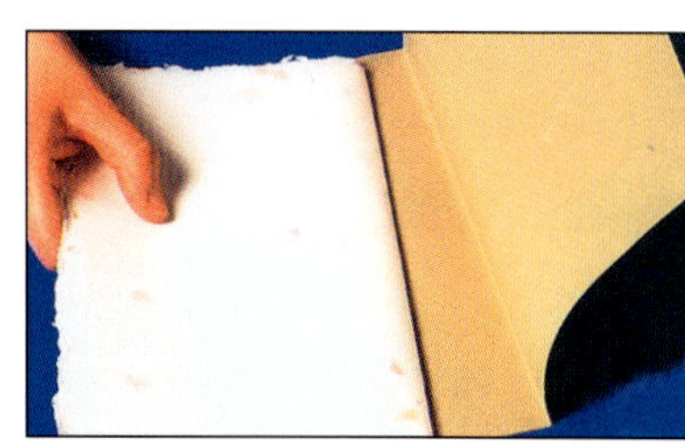

4 Fold the cover in half, and crease the fold with a bone folder. Place the section, together with the vellum flyleaf, into the cover.

5 Use clips to clamp the cover to the section. Using a ruler and a pencil, mark two holes 1¾ in. (4.5 cm) from the head and tail of the book. Mark a center hole with a pencil.

TIP: *If the clips make creases in the paper, fold a scrap of paper and place it between the clip and the book, to protect the book.*

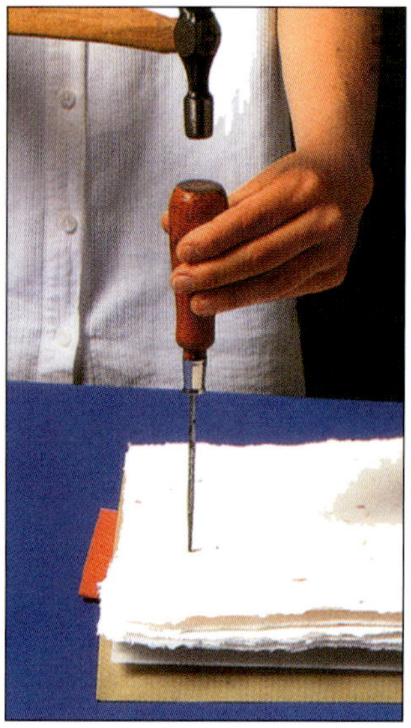

6 Pierce the three holes from the inside of the book using an awl and hammer.

7 Using three strands of green embroidery thread, thread a bookbinder's needle. Begin sewing by entering the center hole from the outside of the book. Pull the thread through, leaving 4 in. (10 cm) of thread on the outside of the book.

8 Enter the bottom hole and pull the thread through to the outside of the book. Enter the center hole and pull the thread to the inside. Enter the top hole and pull the thread through. Ensure that the thread is taut all along the spine.

9 On the exterior of the spine, tie a double knot. Trim the threads to equal lengths.

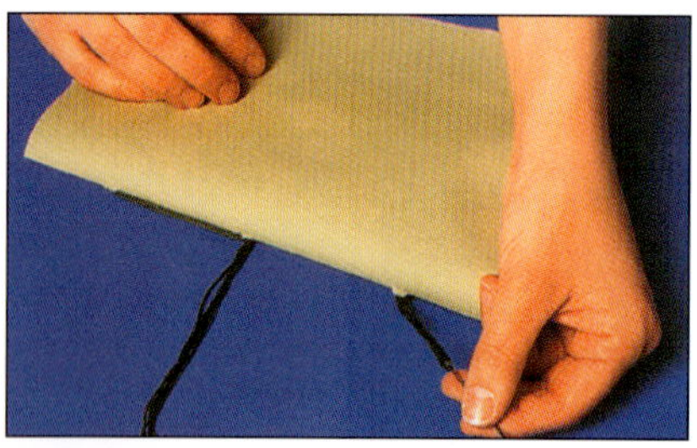

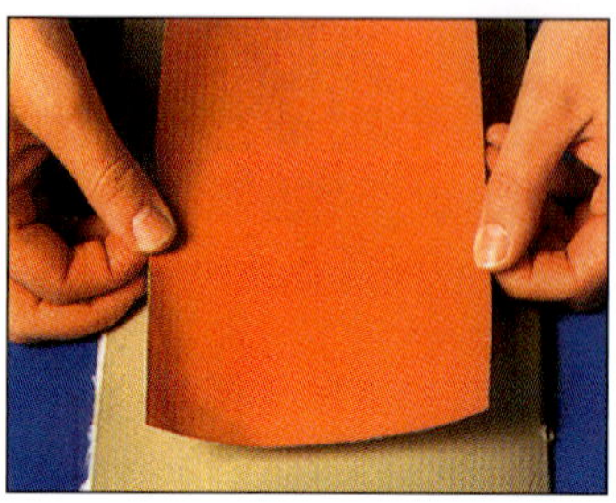

10 Cut a piece of contrasting paper to 4½ in. (11 cm) wide by 7 in. (18 cm) long. Here, we used a rust-colored paper stock. Glue this to the front of the book cover.

11 Apply a thin layer of glue to a preserved leaf.

12 Position the leaf in the center of the rust paper, pointing from corner to corner. Gently smooth in place.

ABOVE: *Here is another example of a single-section book made from handmade paper. A shell on the end of a linen thread forms the closure for this little book.*

Accordion Scrapbook

Accordion books are widely used in the Far East and this book has an exotic Eastern feel with the black feather contrasting against the deep gold cover and bamboo leaves embedded in the pages.

1 Cut two rectangles 10 x 4¾ in. (25 x 12 cm) from the cardboard for the covers. Cut two sheets of gold cover paper, slightly smaller.

2 Using craft glue, stick the cover paper to the outside of the cardboard covers. Smooth them down using the bone folder.

3 Stick the feather to the front cover with craft glue. Place a telephone directory or heavy book on top and leave until dry.

4 Cut four lengths of black bias tape about 20 in. (50 cm) long. Glue these to the inside covers to run across the width in parallel pairs 2½ in. (6.5 cm) from the top and bottom.

5 Cut a long strip of handmade paper 24 x 9 in. (60 x 23 cm). Increase the length by 4 in. (10 cm) per page for more pages. Mark out intervals 4 in. (10 cm) along the length on both sides.

6 Score and fold on alternate sides so that the paper will fold easily, accordion style.

7 Depending on your usage and paper, you may wish to line these pages by pasting smaller pieces of paper on top. Here, we added handmade paper with roughly torn edges to one side of the book.

8 Cut two lengths of adhesive book-cloth tape 10 in. (25 cm) long and two lengths 4¾ in. (12 cm) for each cover. Faintly mark a ¼ in. (0.6 cm) edging around the outside covers and stick the tape along these borders. Cut corners diagonally for a neat finish.

9 Turn each cover over and cut slits—matching the black tapes—into the sticky tape, using a scalpel. Slot the tapes through the slits. Continue to stick tape along the edge and inside.

10 Attach the ends of the accordion paper to the inside of both covers with craft glue. Glue a strip of binding tape along the edges to cover the joints. Cut corners diagonally for a neat finish. Leave both covers under a heavy book to dry.

It makes a refreshing change when a book opens in an unusual way. This accordion book with its concertina folds is tied together at the side with black binding tape and a stylish feather decorates the front cover.

Floral Fabric Scrapbook

The pages in this book are grouped into sections with floral fabric dividers, making it easy for you to find what you need. Add trimmings with tape, and stitch on buttons or beads.

YOU WILL NEED

Piece of firm cardboard, *26 x 11 in. (66 x 28 cm)*

Craft glue (PVA)

Various cotton fabrics

Lining fabric

Iron-on interfacing and iron

3 sheets thin cardboard, *12 x 8¼ in. (30 x 21 cm)*

20 sheets of card stock, *12 x 8¼ in. (30 x 21 cm)*

Bookcloth tape, 2 in. *(5 cm) wide*

Thick round elastic

Craft knife and metal ruler

Scissors

Bone folder

Awl and paper punch

1 Cut two pieces of cardboard, each 13 x 8¼ in. (33 x 21 cm) and two strips sized 13 x ¾ in. (33 x 2 cm) using a metal ruler and craft knife.

2 Pair each strip with the larger board, leaving a ¾ in. (2 cm) gap between them. Glue each pair together using craft glue and gauze. These "bandaged" gaps will form the hinges of your book.

Use this book as a scrapbook for snippets of favorite material or bits and pieces that evoke a special memory and will inspire your sewing projects.

3 Cut out two pieces of cotton fabric for the covers 16 x 13 in. (40.5 x 33 cm) and two pieces of lining fabric 10¼ x 7 in. (26 x 18 cm). Line each piece with lightweight iron-on interfacing. Remember to cover the interfacing with a cloth when ironing.

4 Apply glue to the outside of the cardboard and place it onto the wrong side of the cover fabric. Turn over and smooth out any air bubbles with a bone folder. Snip the corners to miter them neatly and paste the edge over onto the inside. Repeat with the second cover. Leave to dry under heavy books or telephone directories.

5 Once dry, paste the lining to the inside of each cover. Smooth out any bubbles and leave to dry as before.

6 To make the dividers, cover three sheets of thin cardboard on each side with floral fabric (see Step 4). Using the templates shown here, cut out dividing tabs. Create a flexible edge by taping the bookcloth around the spine edge of each divider, so that it overlaps the edge of the card by 1 in. (2.5 cm).

7 Mark the spine holes on the covers, dividers, and sheets of card stock. These should be ¼ in. (6 mm) from the edge and ¾ in. (2 cm) apart. Use the awl for the covers and dividers, and a paper punch for the card.

8 Compile the pages, inserting the dividers as needed. Bind the spine together by threading thick, round elastic spirally through the holes. Tie a knot in each end to secure.

The elasticated spiral binding allows the book to "bulk out" when fabric and buttons or bows are added. You could add an extra fastener—such as a ribbon—to keep the book shut if it's bursting at the seams.

A Gift from Nature

Returning from a country walk with a collection of nature's weird and wonderful creations is a delightful pastime, and the objects are a source of inspiration. This is a scrapbook designed for you to keep, arrange, and make notes on your finds, for you to dip into yourself or give to a special friend.

The front of this book is decorated with pressed snowdrops lightly glued to the paper. Keep this box in a box to protect it. The book is fastened with a wraparound device and a feather.

YOU WILL NEED

Plain cardboard, *9 x 13 in. (22 x 33 cm)*

Corrugated cardboard, *9 x 13 in. (22 x 33 cm)*

Moss paper, *12 x 15 in. (30 x 38 cm)*

Paper glue

Raffia

Handmade paper, *8 x 12 in. (20 x 30 cm)*

Rubber band

Treasury tag paper fasteners *(string with a brad at each end)*

Feather and shell

Hole punch

Awl

1 Using a craft knife (scalpel) and metal ruler, cut out the following rectangles: From plain cardboard and corrugated cardboard 9 x 13 in. (22 x 33 cm); from moss paper 12 x 15 in. (30 x 38 cm). Score parallel lines 1¾ in. (4.5 cm) apart down the center of the plain cardboard using a pointed implement, such as an awl or a craft knife (scalpel).

2 Stick two-sided tape round all four edges on the unscored side of the plain cardboard. Lay the moss paper wrong side up and place the scored side of the cardboard on top. Snip into the corners of the moss paper and fold over the edges, attaching them to the tape.

3 Attach a piece of raffia at least 18 in. (45 cm) long to the center back edge of the plain cardboard. Then glue this board to the flat (reverse) side of the corrugated cardboard. Bend along the scored lines to form the book's shape. Pierce two holes at the back of the book, 3 in. (8 cm) apart and ½ in. (1 cm) from the spine.

4 Thread one end of a treasury tag paper fastener through each hole. The brad (or bar) on the end will anchor along a groove of the corrugated cardboard.

For the insides, handmade-paper pages are fastened with treasury tags. The book is filled with collage patches, glued and sewn into place, and small envelopes fixed with craft glue and finally decorated with feathers.

5 Fold a sheet of handmade or similar paper in half to make a sheet 6 x 8 in. (15 x 20 cm) and use a hole punch to make a hole centered along the folded edge.

6 Thread enough of these pages onto the treasury tag paper fasteners to fill the spine of the book and hold them securely with a tightly looped rubber band.

7 Allowing enough raffia to wrap right around the book, tie a shell with a hole in it (or something similar) to the end and cut off the excess.

8 Wrap this tie around the book, and where the raffia overlaps, secure it with a feather. Arrange pressed flowers and glue them onto suitable paper. Affix this collage to the front of the book with glue or two-sided tape.

Suede Splendor

Made from soft, supple suede and special Khadi paper in shades of brown and russet, this stylish book just begs to be used. Continue the organic theme by recording nature notes in it or displaying pressed flowers or leaves. Use new suede or old—try recycling suede from an old jacket or skirt.

YOU WILL NEED

Piece of suede, *34 x 22 in. (87 x 56 cm)*

Khadi paper, *about 21 sheets, 10½ x 8 in. (27 x 20 cm)*

Button thread

Beeswax

Suede thonging

Duffle coat toggle

Pencil

Ruler

Awl

Leather or darning needle

Scissors

1 Fold the suede in half widthwise (leather side facing up), and lightly mark a pencil line down the center.

2 From this line make seven lines either side, each ¼ in. (6 mm) apart.

3 Mark out points along each line, midway and 1¼ in. (3 cm) from the top and bottom. Make holes using the awl. This will form the spine.

4 Fold each sheet of Khadi paper in half, leaving its natural deckle-edging intact. Nestle three folded sheets inside each other. Make seven of these "signatures."

5 Mark points along the paper to match the spine holes (see Step 3). Thread the needle and draw a long piece of button thread through the beeswax. Take one paper signature and align it with the seven pencil lines on the inside of the suede cover. Stitch from inside the pages through the suede. At the top hole run the thread along the outside of the cover.

6 Insert the needle back through the cover at the bottom hole, across the inside pages, and out through the center hole. Take the needle around the previous stitch and back through the hole.

7 Tie the ends of thread together with a square knot (left over right, and right over left) and trim the ends. Repeat with the remaining six segments.

Khadi paper is a roughly textured handmade paper with natural deckle-edging, available from good arts and crafts stores. Used here, it enhances the book's organic look and feel.

LEFT: *Khadi papers*

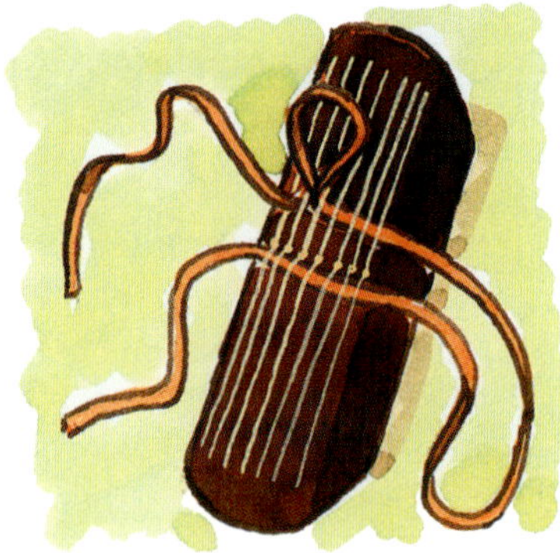

8 Measure and cut a length of thonging to wrap around the book two and a half times.

9 Double it and thread the ends, from the back, under the spine stitches either side of the center. Leave the loop projecting from the back cover to act as the buttonhole.

10 Tie the toggle into place at the edge of the front cover. Button up the book to get the correct length before snipping off excess.

Collect items from a walk in the countryside to put in your beautiful suede-covered scrapbook.

Buttonhole Book

The final project in this section is a delightful little book with a surprise binding feature. This is sure to become a favorite of yours and a coveted gift for a friend. The end result is well worth the careful measuring and cutting.

YOU WILL NEED

72 sheets of cream paper, *4¼ x 8½ in. (10.8 x 21.5 cm)*

Bone folder

Brick wrapped in paper, *as a weight*

Clip

Craft knife

Steel ruler

Cutting mat

Sheet of purple card, *4½ x 9 in. (11.5 x 22.8 cm)*

Pencil

Bookbinder's needle

Waxed white embroidery thread

White acrylic paint

Rubber star stamp

Sponge

1 Sort the sheets of cream paper into nine sets of eight sheets each. Jog the edge of one set, and fold it in half using a bone folder. Repeat with the remaining sets. Position the sections in a stack and place under a weight for three or four hours. Clip the sections together; trim the fore-edge using a craft knife and a metal ruler.

2 Mark a ½ in. (1.5 cm) spine in the center of the purple card stock. Mark and cut out a box in the center of the cover, measuring 2 in. (5 cm) wide and 3 in. (7.5 cm) high. This box will form the buttonhole of the book cover.

3 Score the spine and fold it into the cover.

4 Remove the sections from under the weight and place them inside the cover. Using a pencil, mark the edge of the buttonhole on the sections.

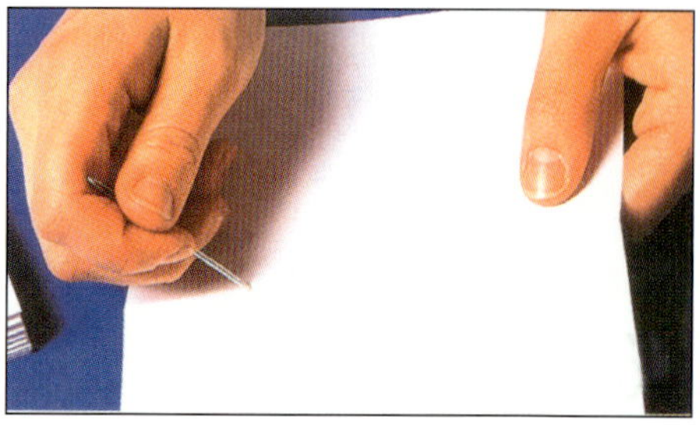

5 Remove the sections from the book cover and pierce the holes where marked with a bookbinder's needle.

6 Thread a bookbinder's needle with waxed embroidery thread. Enter the hole at the tail of the book from inside and pull the thread to the outside. Leave 2 in. (5 cm) of thread inside the book. Wrap the thread around the tail of the buttonhole cover and tie the thread with the end inside the book. Tie a double knot over the hole.

7 Exit the hole at the tail of the book, and add a second section by entering the same hole of the next section.

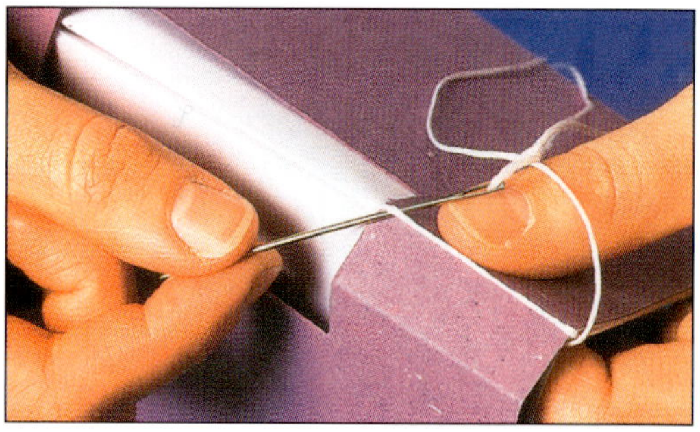

8 Loop the thread around the tail of the buttonhole cover and link it into the thread of the first section. Continue adding sections in the same manner until they have all been added.

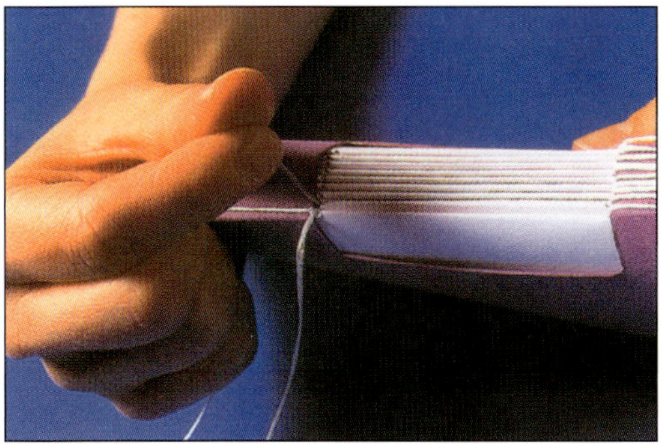

9 Sew the sections to the head of the book by following steps 6 to 8.

10 Apply white acrylic paint to a rubber star stamp with a sponge, then stamp a white star on the front cover. Lift up the stamp carefully to reveal the image.

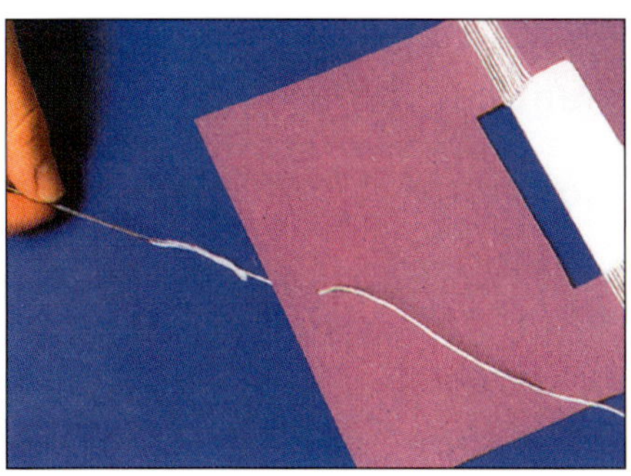

11 Pierce a hole in the center edge of the front and back covers, and thread two pieces of white embroidery thread through both holes. Tie the threads together in a bow for a decorative closure.

CUTTING A RECESS

1 Cut your cover boards to the required size, adding ⅛ in. (3 mm) at the head, tail, and fore-edge. Decide how long you want the tapes to be, then cut them to the desired length.

2 Place the boards on the book and the tapes in position, then mark the width and length of the tapes on the boards with a pair of dividers. Remove the board.

3 Using a craft knife and safety ruler, cut and peel away the area of board between the divider points to the depth of the tape.

4 Coat the boards with PVA glue and cover with paper or cloth, making sure the covering material is pushed down well into the recesses. Fold, cut, and glue down the corners and turn-ins and leave the covered boards between waxed paper and pressing boards under a weight to dry.

HOUSE AND GARDEN

Considering how much time we spend in and around our homes, we rarely remember to record day-to-day events. In this section we set out to put this right, so that all that hard work both indoors and out is recorded for posterity. First is Ideal Home, a scrapbook into which you can put ideas and pictures cut from magazines to help you conjure up the house of your dreams. There are also suggestions on how to record working progress, so that you can keep a record of before and after.

Ideal Home Book

Decorating or redecorating your home can present you with a bewildering array of choices, so it is useful to keep a scrapbook in which you can jot down ideas, color notes, measurements, and so on. You can also use it to build up a library of inspirational interiors clipped from magazines or newspapers, along with samples of fabric and wallpaper, and other handy information about prices or the names of suppliers.

This book is designed as a folder into which you can add more pages to create the house of your dreams.

YOU WILL NEED

Foam board (polyboard)

Sheet of clear acetate

Construction paper

Strips of balsa wood, *¼ in. (5 mm) diameter, half-round (C-section)*

Small cans of emulsion paint

Glue gun and glue sticks

Glass-headed pins

Binding clip

Dowel rod

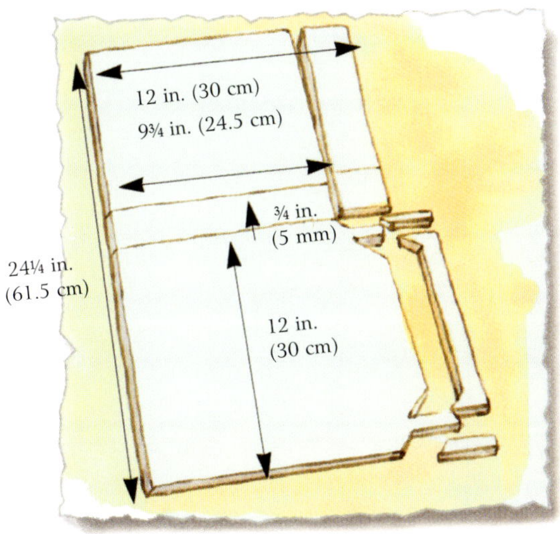

1 Cut the foam board to measure 12 x 24¼ in. (30 x 61.5 cm). Score down to the bottom layer of cardboard 12 in. (30 cm) in from one edge from top to bottom, then another ¼ in. (5 mm) in to make the spine of the book, as shown. Cut the back and spine down to 9¾ in. (24.5 cm) in height, and draw the outline of the roof and chimneys on the front, following the diagram carefully. Cut out the shape using the ruler and craft knife.

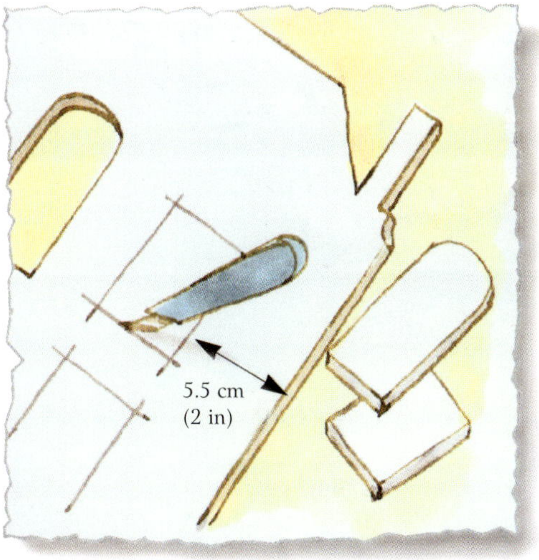

2 Mark all the windows, including the fanlight above the door. The windows are 2 in. (5.5 cm) from the side edges. Cut out the windows, holding the craft knife at a 90° angle to the board, and remove them from the front. Cut partway through the panels on the front door, making sure that you do not cut through the board.

3 Mark and cut out two strips of decorative masonry measuring ½ x 9 in. (1.5 x 23 cm) from the cut-away foam board, as shown.

4 Paint the door and masonry strips in a color that will contrast with the rest of the house. Paint the entire board, front and insides, or the structure will warp and curve.

5 When the paint is dry, glue the sheet of clear acetate inside the front of the book to make the windows. Then cut a piece of construction paper exactly the same size as the whole book. Mark the position of the windows and cut them out. Fold the lines of the spine carefully and glue the paper to the inside of the book.

6 Cut strips of balsa wood to make windowpanes and sills. In addition, cut two lengths to run along the top of the house, two shorter pieces to make the triangle above the arched window, and three more strips for the triangle around the fanlight. To make the pillars by the side of the door and the decoration at the top of the house, cut pieces of half round (C-section) wooden dowel rod ¼ in. (5 mm) diameter to the appropriate lengths. Paint all these pieces white and, when they are dry, glue them in place along with the decorative masonry panels.

7 Draw the tiles on the roof and the brickwork on the chimneys, then carefully cut partway through the pencil lines with the craft knife. Paint the roof with gray watercolor paint and the chimneys brick red. Cut the top from the glass-headed pin and paint it gold; glue it to the center of the door to make the knob.

In the future this book will be an interesting example of the design of its era. It will be fun to compare it with photographs of your "finished" home.

8 To complete the book, glue the binding clip in position on the inside back of the book, using a hot glue gun. Pages can be punched and threaded onto the binding clip as desired.

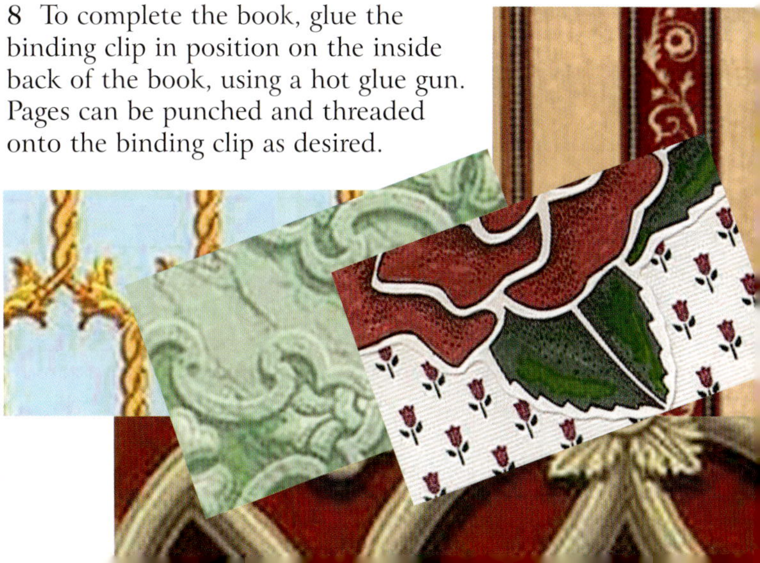

Garden Scrapbook

Make a note of where you've planted bulbs in this practical little book and also keep snippets of information about plant varieties to grow next year. Divided into three sections—flowers, vegetables, and fruits—there's a keepsake envelope attached to the inside front and back covers where you can keep seeds, leaves, or flowers.

YOU WILL NEED

Spiral bound notebook with colored dividers

Aluminum or pewter foil, 1/16 *in. (1 mm) thick*

Double-sided carpet tape

Small envelopes

Ruler

Tracing (transfer) paper

Ballpoint pen

Adhesive tape

Scissors

1 Measure your book cover and trace a design from a book or magazine with tracing paper. Cut some aluminum foil to the same size, and place it on a soft cloth or mouse mat. Cover with the tracing, and secure with adhesive tape. Trace over the image with a ballpoint pen, pressing firmly.

LEFT: *Transform an ordinary notebook into a special place for your gardening tips and bits. It is very easy to personalize the book with an aluminum plaque and page dividers.*

2 Cover the back of the foil with double-sided carpet tape. Cut out the image using general purpose scissors.

3 Choose a design for each divider tab. Trace as for Step 1 and transfer to stock card. Cover the back of the tabs with double-sided tape and cut them out.

4 Cut card stock in the same shape as the tabs, but ⅛ in. (3 mm) shorter. Peel the backing off the tape and attach the card to the tab backs, leaving the ends uncovered.

5 Divide the book into three equal sections. Place an adhesive tab end on each section, lining up the card with the edge of the page. Press firmly in position. Stick the cover design in place. Stick attractive envelopes to the inside front and back covers.

Before and After

When all the work is done, and there's time to sit back and relax, it's good to reflect on what you have achieved. Most of us don't think to take photos of our home until all the decorating is finished and it's looking great, but the trick is to record your labors right from the start.

Collage together decorating and renovating photographs to give the feeling of work in progress.

1 If you have before and after photos of your house, you can color photocopy and enlarge them. Have them laminated at a print and photocopy store, to form the covers of your scrapbook. Sandwich colored sheets of art board between the laminated house pictures and have the scrapbook spiral bound.

2 To take a panoramic photograph of a scene, first mark your foot position with masking tape. Turn slowly around the room, making sure that each shot you take slightly overlaps the last. Check that you did not move from your position.

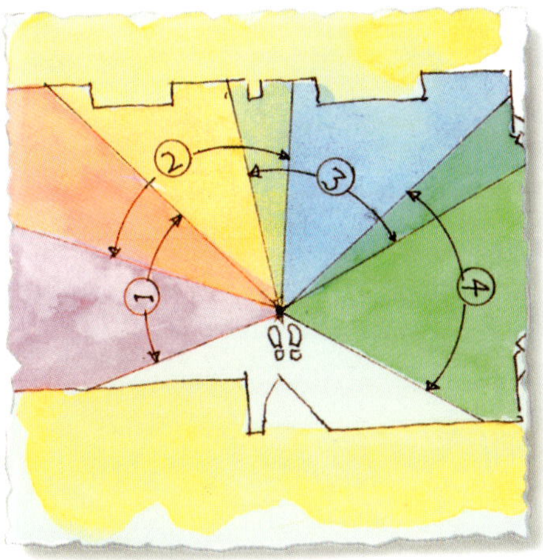

3 Place your photographs in sequence and play around with them to get the best arrangement. Check that the montage will fit onto the page. Draw a plan of your chosen arrangement for reference.

4 Cover your work area with newsprint to protect it, and spray the back of each photograph with photographic mountng spray.

5 Once the montage is completed, clean it with a soft cloth and place a heavy weight over the image until it is dry.

Gardening Keepsakes

Earthy handmade papers and gardening twine give this project a feeling of the great outdoors. Gardening has become such a popular leisure activity that it won't be difficult to find a wonderful choice of wrapping paper on garden themes to decorate your pages. You can include seed packets and details of sewing and planting as a reminder of how your garden grows.

Instead of using corner mounts, echo the flower details in photographs by gluing cut-out flowers to the pages to hold your pictures in place.

YOU WILL NEED

Mat board (mounting card)
33 x 23 in. (84 x 57.5 cm)

2 thin scrapbooks or 1 thick scrapbook, with soft covers

Contrasting sheets of handmade paper in earth/plant colors

Gardening twine

Floral giftwrap, seed catalogs, old gardening magazines

Cutting mat

Awl

1 Remove the covers of two blank scrapbooks and cut the books in half to form the pages. Tape the four halves together along their spines. Be sure the pages are all the same size; trim them with a craft knife and ruler if necessary.

2 Cut one piece of mat board (mounting card) for the back and cover that will protect the trimmed pages, allowing ½ in. (1 cm) on all sides. Cut lines partway through the mat board to form the spine.

3 Fold the mat board along the spine. Cut off a square of the front cover, leaving approximately 2 in. (5 cm) along the edge of the cover for the binding.

4 Insert the scrapbook pages into the binding/back cover unit and use an awl to make holes through the front binding and trimmed pages, but not the back cover. Place a piece of wood between the back cover and trimmed pages to protect the back cover.

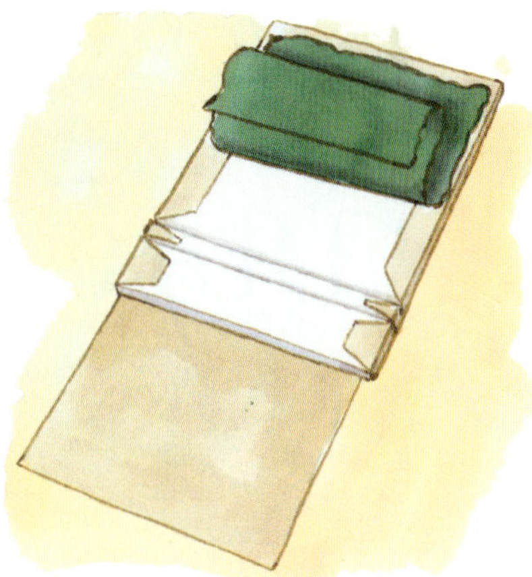

5 Cut a single sheet of heavyweight handmade paper big enough to cover the outside of the book—front, back, and binding. Square the edges of the front section and make it slightly smaller than the back—the square of cover board cut off in Step 3 will be attached to it. Punch holes through the covering paper to match those on the binding strip. Use a piece of heavyweight handmade paper to line the inside of the back cover and spine.

6 Cover the square of front-cover board with contrasting lightweight handmade paper.

Your album can record how your plants grow over the years, with details of gardening gifts from friends, and seed packets to remind you of the plant names.

7 Thread gardening twine or string through the holes in the front binding and the trimmed pages (see Step 4) and tie the ends in a bow. Leave a very small gap along the edge of the binding and glue the covered square of board onto the paper on the front of the book. Decorate the cover as desired, using motifs cut from catalogs, magazines, or wrapping paper.

IDEAS FOR THE INSIDE

ABOVE RIGHT: *Paper collage lends itself to work of a decorative nature. This busy design layers stenciled motifs and patterns torn freehand over blocks of handpainted paper. The end result is this richly colored background for the paper pansies.*

Cut out flowers from wrapping paper or magazines to decorate the pages or to hold your photographs in place. You could choose blooms that appear in the photos.

Use papers similar to those decorating the cover to make borders or to frame your pictures on the page.

More Ideas

A home is much more than just bricks and mortar. Here are ideas for celebrating two key aspects of many homes—the garden and the family.

Toward the end of the summer, collect a selection of flowers from your garden and press them in a press if you possess one. In this book by Carole Thorpe-Gunner she used a small block of watercolor paper which she tore roughly and then brushed with a coat of bright yellow watercolor paint to make the pages. The fading colors of the pressed flowers stood out well against the bright background. The backbone of the book is a budding twig with a piece of soft thin leather, threaded in a bodkin and pushed through each page. This held the book together and the ends were wrapped around each side.

This scrapbook is for animal lovers. The cover was inspired by a charming drawing of a cat done by a six-year-old boy. The image was enlarged and the shape cut from yellow felt which was stitched onto the cover fabric. The cat's tail wraps around the book and acts as a closure with snaps underneath. Inside you can mount drawings and images of your favorite pet, held together visually with rubber stamps and glued-on sequins. This would be a great project to do with your children.

Fishing Folder

This scrapbook would be an ideal present for someone who loves fishing. It can be used to record prize catches and making notes of where and when the fish were caught, together with a photograph or two. It is a reasonably simple idea that can be adapted to suit any hobby or craft of your choice.

For a woodworker you could choose a picture of someone sawing, bordered with a wood- or brick-effect dolls' house wallpaper. Then glue a miniature hammer and nails onto the cover.

YOU WILL NEED

Foam board (polyboard)

Green baize fabric or moss paper, *textured paper with a "nap" of green nylon on one side, which can be obtained from stores and mail-order houses that carry handmade paper*

Wrapping paper

Plastic fish

Darning needle and strong darning thread

Brown paper

1 Cut a piece of foam board 8½ x 13 in. (21.5 x 33 cm). Cut parallel lines partway through the board, ½ in. (1 cm) apart, halfway along the top of the board to make the spine. Remove the top two layers, leaving the base cardboard along the spine. Cut out a window measuring 3¼ x 4½ in. (8 x 11 cm), centered on one side of the board, as shown.

2 Glue the board to the reverse side of a piece of moss paper 10¼ x 14½ in. (25.5 x 36 cm) and leave it to dry. Cut a small window from the moss paper, allowing a ¾ in. (2 cm) overlap around the window in the board. Snip off the outer corners of the moss paper. Fold over the margins of the moss paper and glue them to the inside of the board. Cut diagonal lines in the moss paper overlap up to the window edges of the board and fold back and glue the overlap in place.

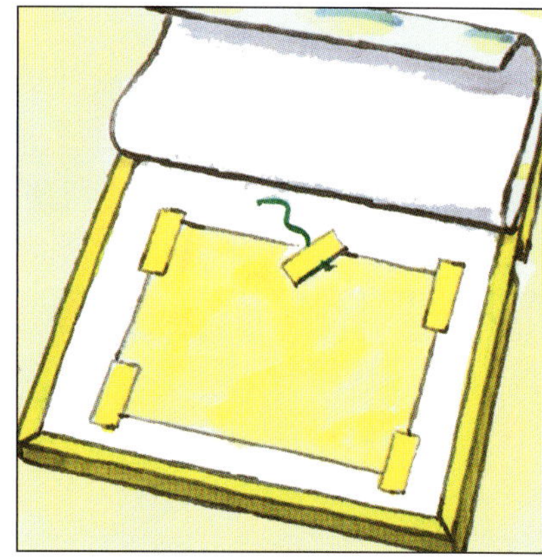

3 Choose a suitable picture to fit inside the window and tape it in position, then cover the entire inside cover with suitable wrapping paper, such as the fish-pattern paper used here. Place the entire cover under a weight until it is dry. Bend the book into shape and glue a suitable motif like this fish to the front cover. Here, a "fishing line" has been stitched through from the fish to the rod, using a needle and strong thread.

4 To make the pages, fold three groups of paper measuring 8¼ x 12½ in. (21 x 31 cm), using five sheets in each group.

5 Stitch each group of pages through the center and through the spine of the book, using a needle and double-lengths of strong darning thread. Tie the ends in a bow inside each group of pages.

JUN
MAY
APR
MAR

THE TEENAGE YEARS

At this most hectic and exciting time of their lives, our children are so occupied living life to the full that they don't have time to record it. However, it is nice to have a book of memories to look back on, and the projects in this section are fun and simple to make. These scrapbooks span the teenage years from the early teens right through to graduation from college. Once compiled these books will give a fascinating insight into some of the memories and experiences, both happy and sad, that your teenagers experienced.

College Days

Here is a way of saving those favorite old denim jeans—use them to cover a ring binder or folder to keep mementos in. The pages provide the space for keeping memorable essays, photographs, collages made from cards, items given to you by special friends, ticket stubs—in fact the list is endless.

The safest way of attaching a diary is to use a keyring on a spring so that if it escapes from the pocket it won't get lost.

YOU WILL NEED

An old pair of jeans

Two-ring notebook or folder

Seam ripper

1 Cut off the legs of the old jeans and unpick the seams below the front fastening, on the inside leg and the front of the crotch. The result should closely resemble the illustration above.

2 Cut a section from a remaining leg and attach to the inside of the notebook, making slits to slip the metal rings through. Stick the denim in place with two-sided tape.

3 Press the opened-out jeans and line up the top of the waistband with the top edge of the notebook. Make sure the back pocket is in a good position on the front of the notebook, then attach the top with two-sided tape, wrapping the side edges around to the inside of the book and secure with two-sided tape. At this point the bottom edge will be loose and baggy.

4 Stitch along the top to join the edges of the waistband on the outside and inside at both back and front.

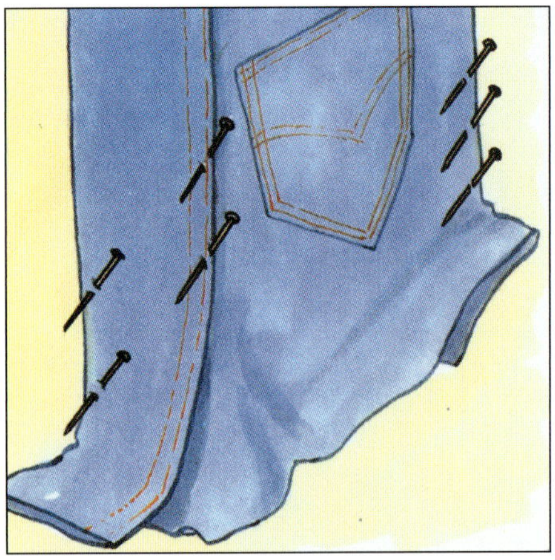

Make the pockets into little time capsules by storing notebooks, letters, and other keepsakes such as sweet wrappers in them.

5 Fold in the excess fabric in the seat of the jeans making a dart along the spine, and another along the bottom half of the front and back edges. Pin to hold the position if necessary.

6 Stitch along the front and back edges to secure these darts.

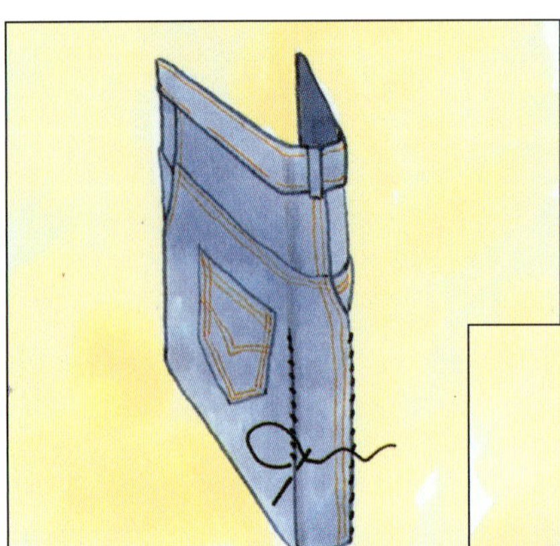

7 Stitch the dart along the spine on both sides.

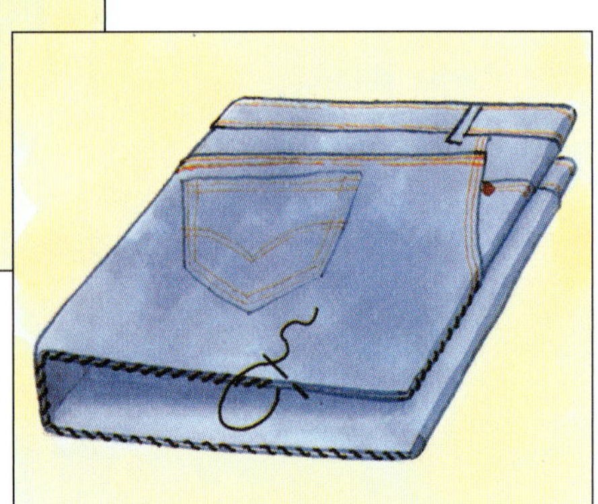

8 Hem the fabric along the bottom edge, using appropriately colored thread, to finish the notebook.

Most students nowadays have access to a computer and they may prefer to play around and make a book cover using computer collage. Multiple layering techniques have been used to create this work by Richard Holloway, which features ancient and modern themes inspired by Eastern and Egyptian cultures. It is a combination of images taken with a digital camera and photodisc with a series of subtly colored collected images.

Dream Catcher

Wired-up plastic tubing and translucent plastic combine to make this unusual book a special place to catch your dreams. With its "glow-in-the-dark" star, it will be easy to find at night to record your very latest dream.

YOU WILL NEED

3 sheets of translucent plastic or acetate *11 x 11 in. (28 x 28 cm)*

Blue/green/mauve notepad *8 x 8 in. (20 x 20 cm)*

Galvanized garden wire, *18 in. (45 cm)*

Wide plastic tubing *¼ in. (6 mm)*

Craft glue (PVA)

2 large beads

Large fluorescent star

Matt silver foil

Double-sided carpet tape

Scissors

Ruler and pencil

Masking tape

2 thin strips of wood *8 x ¾ in. (20 x 1.5 cm)*

2 G-clamps

Drill *with ¼ in. (6 mm) spur bit*

Thick dowel rod

1 Cut three plastic sheets with scissors as follows.

Back cover: 8 x 8 in. (20 x 20 cm). Divider: Same size as first, but cut away a ¾ in. (2 cm) border on three sides. Front cover: Same size as back cover, but cut away a 1¼ in. (3 cm) border on three sides.

2 Place the three sheets on top of each other, lining them up at the left edge where the spiral tubing will be. Make sure the borders are even around the other three sides. Secure with masking tape. Mark points for drilling holes at ¾ in. (2 cm) intervals. Mark the same points on the pad and on one of the battens.

3 Tape the pad and plastic sheets, lining up all the markings. Clamp them between the battens with the marked points on top. Drill the holes.

4 Insert the wire through the plastic tubing (available from hardware or aquarium stores). Drill a hole in the end of a dowel rod and mark ¾ in. (2 cm) intervals. Insert wire into the hole and wrap the tubing around the stick to make a spiral coil to the required length.

5 Split the notepad in half and insert the plastic divider. Add the front and back covers. Line up all the holes and insert the plastic tubing in the holes, carefully winding it on. Trim off excess tubing, leaving ¾ in. (2 cm) of wire at each end. Bend these into right angles and glue a bead onto each end.

6 Decorate the front of the pad with the glowing star. Back the silver foil with double-sided carpet tape and cut into little squares. Stick around the inside of the back plastic cover so that they show through as a border.

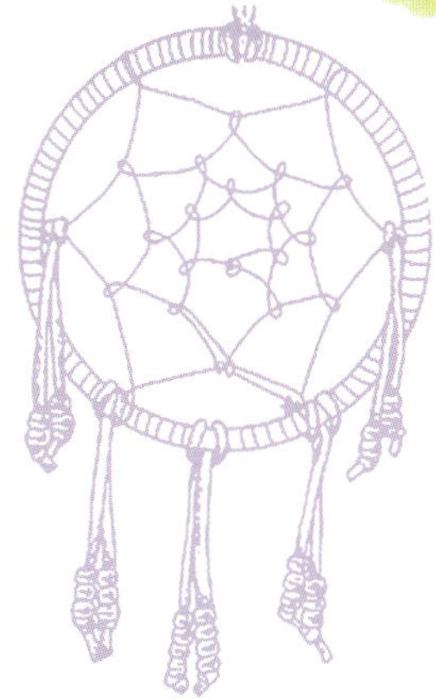

Fun and Frolics

This brightly colored and cheerful scrapbook is easy to make and once it is finished you can simply slide your photographs, ticket stubs, and other keepsakes under the raffia grids with no glue or tape necessary. The envelopes can be filled with letters, extra photographs, and other similar mementos, but make sure the items are not too bulky or the envelopes may tear.

YOU WILL NEED

A pack of multicolored corrugated cardboard, *12 x 16 in. (30 x 40 cm)*

A 8-in. (20-cm) square of plain cardboard

Bright-colored envelopes

Darning needle

Raffia and raffia fringe

For an alternative front cover decoration you could use an appropriate greeting card attached with glue or two-sided tape.

1 Choose a sheet of corrugated cardboard for the cover and decorate it using photographs wrapped with raffia fringe. Stick the square of plain cardboard to the front cover with two-sided tape and then add the fringed photos in a pleasing arrangement.

2 To make the pages with grids, use raffia in a darning needle to stitch parallel diagonal lines 3 in. (7.5 cm) apart in one direction across a sheet of corrugated cardboard, then repeat in the other direction. Repeat to make eight pages.

3 Stack the pages in order, with the corrugated sides facing each other, and join them together by cross stitching along one long edge, using raffia in a darning needle.

4 On the reverse side of the corrugated pages, stick on bright-colored envelopes with two-sided tape.

Funky Scrapbook

The main ingredients for constructing this fun scrapbook are multi-colored poster boards, wrapping paper, and greeting cards. The covers are made from cardboard covered with wrapping paper, sandwiched between two sheets of clear acetate and joined together through eyelet holes.

YOU WILL NEED

2 pieces of cardboard, 10 x 16 in. (24 x 40 cm) (A3)

4 sheets of clear acetate, 10 x 16 in. (24 x 40 cm) (A3)

12 sheets of multi-colored lightweight poster board (art card), 10 x 16 in. (24 x 40 cm) (A3)

Wrapping paper

Greeting cards, old magazines, etc.

Cord or ribbon

Hole punch

Eyelet maker and eyelets

1 Cover both pieces of cardboard with wrapping paper and decorate each side differently with motifs from greeting cards, old magazines, etc. When the glue is dry, sandwich each board between two sheets of clear acetate.

2 Make eyelet holes in one corner at a time. Insert an eyelet in each hole and clamp it closed. Continue making eyelet holes evenly spaced around the edges of the boards.

3 Punch two holes in each sheet of poster board to correspond with two of the eyelet holes on the left-hand side of the front cover. Tie the covers and pages together with cord or ribbon threaded through the eyelet holes. Knot it securely, but loosely enough to allow the pages to turn easily.

Gothic-style Diary

A clasp inspired by medieval jewelry and richly painted endpapers turns this standard diary into a personal, gothic-style book that you will enjoy writing in every day.

The clasp itself is made from twisted copper wire and upholstery nails (with most of the pin cut off) on a base of thin card and the strap is made from two layers of bookcloth painted the same colors as the clasp. The back of the clasp and strap are then lined with felt and attached to the board with glue and silk and thread. An extension to the design is embossed on the cover board using shaped scraps of grayboard. Of course, you can experiment with brass or silver wire, colored glass, or old pieces of jewelry; and the design of the clasp can be simple and elegant with just a few twists of wire or highly wrought like the one in this project.

YOU WILL NEED

Grayboard

Bookcloth

Paper for pages

Decorated endpapers

Linen sewing thread

Mull

Craft paper

Thin card

Materials for clasp

Acrylic paints

Copper wire

Felt to match or contrast with the backcloth

Waxed paper

PVA glue

Wheatflour paste

Matching Velcro

Knife (scalpel)

Metal ruler

Cutting board or mat

Bone folder

Dividers

Glue and paste brushes

Sewing needle

Wire cutters and pliers (optional)

A piece of thick foam, bigger than the size of the cover boards

Press or pressing boards and G-clamps

Hammer (and chisel optional)

1 Fold, cut, press, and sew the pages of the diary.

2 For the clasp cut two pieces of thin card to your desired shape and decide upon the width of the strap—here it is ¾ in. (2 cm). Cut two pieces of cloth twice this width and approximately 4 in. (10 cm) long, then glue them together. Fold both edges around to meet in the center; crease and glue down. Press for a couple of minutes under a weight.

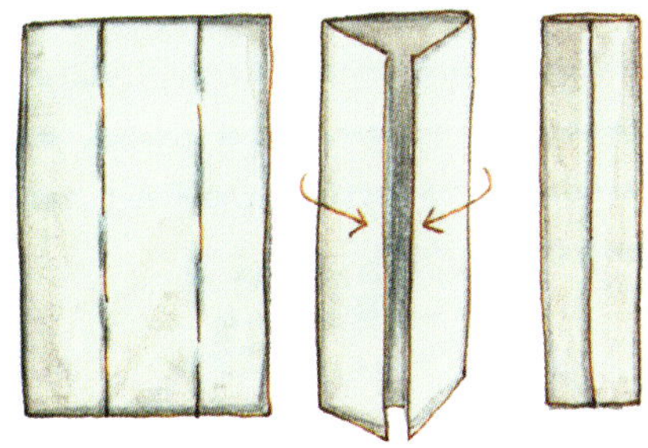

3 Glue the strap to one of the card shapes made in Step 2 (A). Then cut another piece of thin card the same size as (A) but cut to fit around the end of the strap (B). Glue this down. Finally glue the second card shape over the top of (B) so the strap is sandwiched between (C).

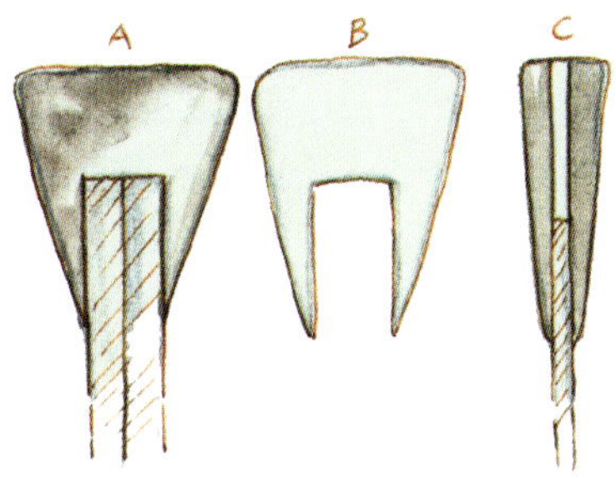

4 Cover the clasp with glued, crumpled paper and wind the wire around and through the shaped board, adding upholstery tacks or whatever you have chosen to use. Paint the clasp and strap with acrylics, then wipe it from the wire. Continue painting and wiping until you have achieved the effect you want.

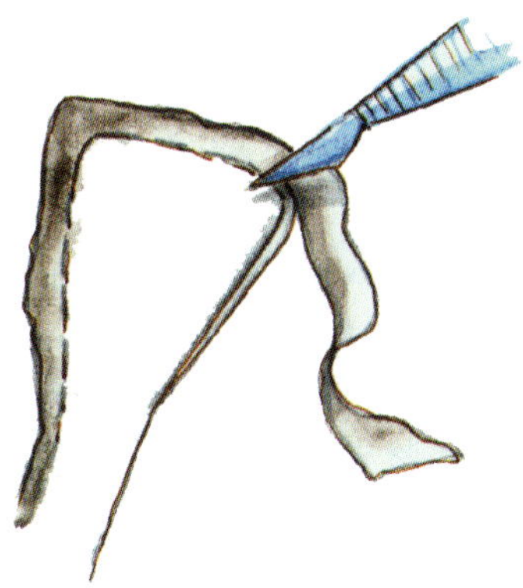

5 Glue a piece of over-sized felt to the back of the clasp and strap and, when the glue is dry, trim the felt to size. Put to one side.

6 Make a pair of decorative endpapers or use commercially printed papers and attach them to the book. To glue the spine, trim the book (if preferred), line the spine and cut the cover boards.

7 Before glueing on the second board, you need to add the cutout shape which forms the raised area. Using the clasp as a pattern, extend the design on to a piece of thin card and cut it out. Glue this shape in position on the front board.

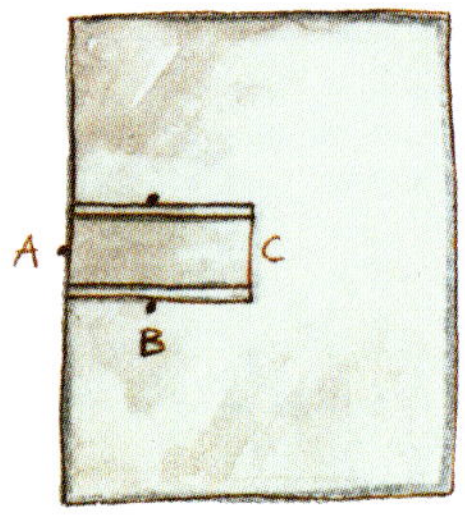

8 So that the strap sits securely and neatly on the back board, it is advisable to cut a recess in the board. To do this, mark the center point of the long edge of the board (A) and position the strap so that the center of it lines up with point (A). Add just under ⅛ in. (3 mm) on each side of the strap and mark with a couple of divider points (B). The recess on the model is 1¾ in. (4.5 cm) long but you can make it longer or slightly shorter, if you wish (C).

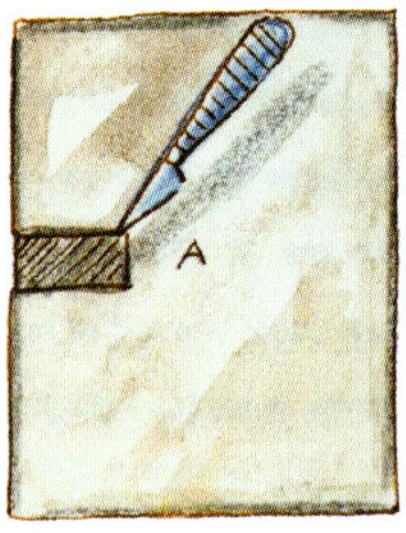

9 Measure the thickness of the strap with the dividers and cut the same thickness of board out of the recess. Using a strong knife, or a hammer and chisel, cut through at point (A) and cut the recess as marked in Step 8.

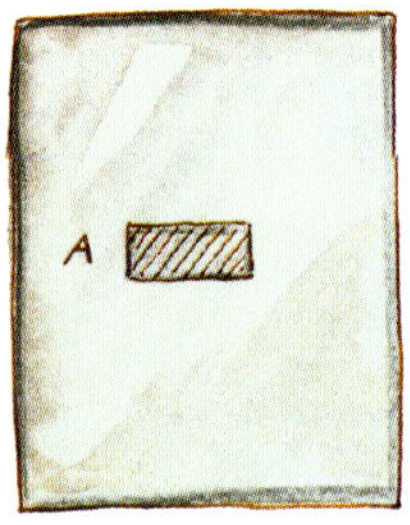

10 Turn the board over and make another recess the same width as before and 1 in. (2.5 cm) long, toward the spine edge, away from the slit (A).

11 Cut your covering cloth ¾ in. (2 cm) bigger all round than the area of the boards and spine. At this stage the cover boards need to be pressed as you glue them. If you don't have a press, you can use pressing boards and two G-clamps. When you have applied the cloth, place the cover board cloth side up on a pressing board (A), lay the foam over the top (B), and cover it with another pressing board (C). Place in the press or between two clamps and tighten until the foam is almost flat. Leave for 10 to 15 minutes. Do this on both front and back boards, attaching the spine piece in the center, and leave it to dry under a weight between waxed paper and pressing boards.

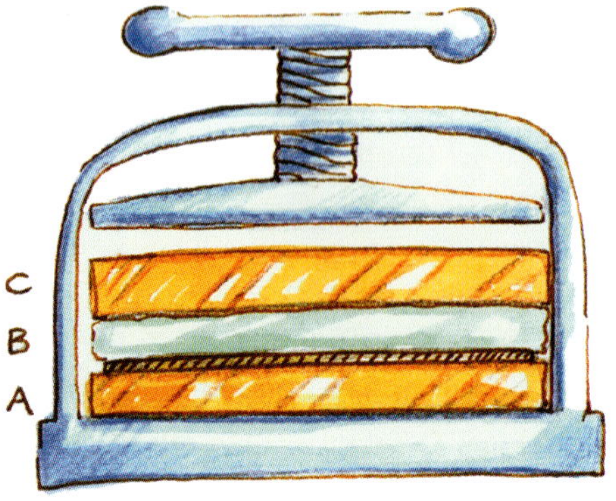

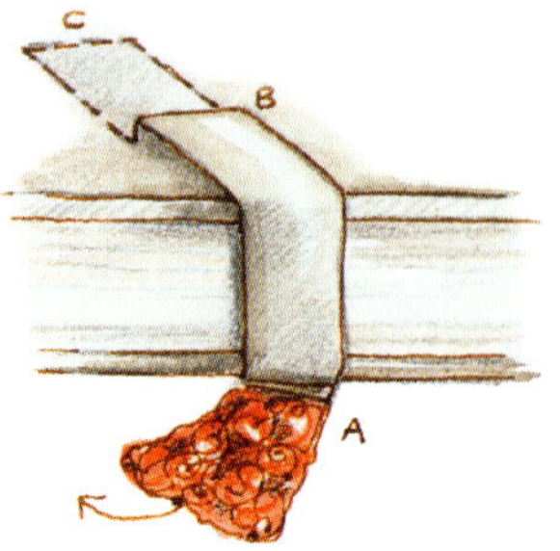

12 Place the pages of the diary prepared in Step 1 in the completed case and measure the required length of the strap. This will be from (A) to (B) to (C) in the diagram. Place the clasp in position, take the strap around the fore-edge of the book and through the slit at (B). Cut the strap to fit into the inner recess, glue, and hammer flat.

13 Glue the strap into the recess on the outside of the board. If you wish, you can add decorative stitches made from silk thread or painted twine, taking them through the board and recessing them on the inside of the board.

14 Trim the mull and the tapes to an equal length and put down the endpapers. Make sure you press the book with the strap undone using the foam or you won't get an even pressing.

15 The next day, when the book is thoroughly dry, glue a small piece of Velcro to the front board and the back of the clasp to act as a fastening. The book is now ready to use.

Fashion Folder

This scrapbook will fire the imagination of any teenager, and provide the perfect place to express their own ideas about art and fashion.

Most teenagers love magazines and if they have trouble throwing them away because of the fashion pictures and hair styles, then this scrapbook is the solution. The book can be divided into different sections so that they can keep a record of all their favorite styles. This particular folder was covered with pink fake fur and a snap fastener was sewed on to close it.

Fancy Felt

Here a loose felt cover, simply stitched, brings a special look to an inexpensive jotter. The endpapers and motif were chosen to complement the design and color scheme.

Beneath this slip-on cover is an ordinary notebook that can be bought from a stationery supplier. The jacket has been made with layers of felt and features a simple leaf shape sewn on with running stitch. It is an ideal little book for students to carry around to keep a record of their classes or just put in the addresses and phone numbers of all their friends.

1 Cut two sheets sized 11½ x 7½ in. (29 x 19 cm) from the endpaper. Paste one sheet over the inside back cover, smoothing in place with the bone folder. Make sure that you work into the groove at the spine. Leave to dry then repeat with inside front cover.

2 Cut a piece 10½ x 6¾ in. (27 x 17 cm) from the black felt. Using pinking shears, cut a piece 10¼ x 6¾ in. (26 x 17 cm) from the dark green felt. Cut a piece 9¾ x 6¼ in. (25.5 x 16 cm) from the light green felt.

3 Make a leaf design template by folding a sheet of paper in half. Then draw a leaf shape using the fold as the center vein and cut out a symmetrical shape.

4 Wrap the light green felt around the notebook. Mark the motif position on the front and back covers. Draw round the leaf, template on the felt and cut out two shapes.

5 Place the light green felt over the dark green, making an even zigzag border. Stitch the felts together around the leaf shapes with light green cotton. Make leaf veins from thick black embroidery thread, each one longer than the leaf and tie a knot in each end. Secure in place with black and green cotton.

6 Place the green leaves on the black felt (this will line the inside front cover). Paste the leaves in position using craft glue. Make veins and stitch them on as before, using light yellow thread.

7 Using a metal ruler and craft knife, cut two parallel lines 6 x 1½ in. (15 x 4 cm) apart down the center of the black felt. Apply a little craft glue to the back of the strip and place it over the cover's spine, between the leaf shapes. Leave to dry.

8 Using pinking shears, cut a strip of dark green felt 6¼ x 1 in. (16 x 2.5 cm) wide and one in black 6 x ½ in. (15 x 1.5 cm). Lay these over the black felt spine. Stitch a green button at the top with light green embroidery thread. Take one straight stitch along the spine, then stitch the other button at the bottom. Take another long stitch back to the top. Tie the thread off on the underside.

9 To make the inside cover, place the black felt in position. Sew a running stitch all around the edge of the cover. Make sure that you allow enough room for your notebook covers to slide in.

10 Fold the covers of the notebook right back and slip them into the felt cover.

Below is another idea for the cover.

Computer File

Store all of your computer documents whether they are on disk or printed out on paper in this innovative plastic file. Round elastic has been threaded onto the front of the folder, creating a secure place to store disks. To personalize this folder, include your favorite pictures in the special picture frames which have been cut out of the side using a craft knife.

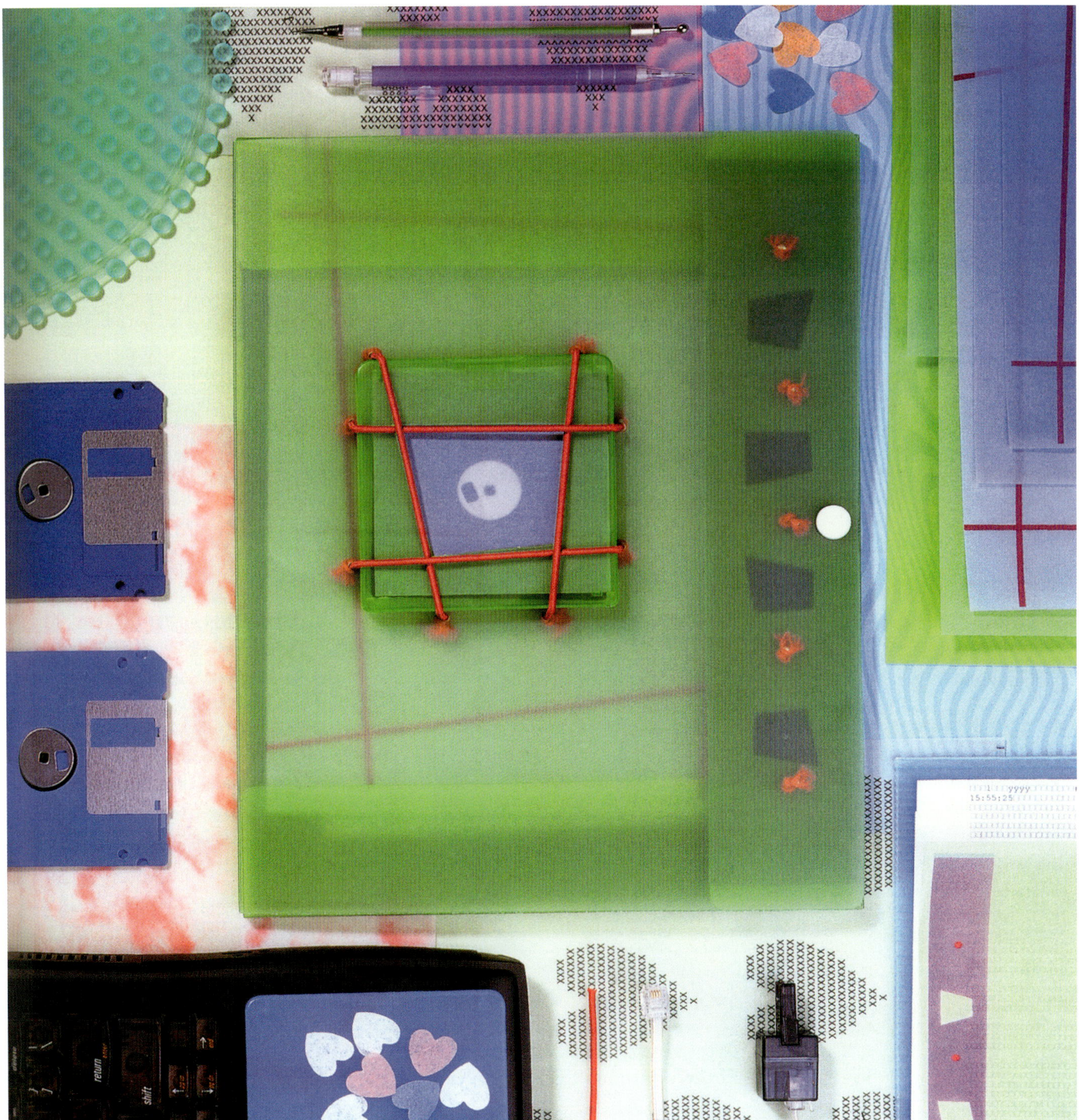

School Years

This scrapbook is for keeping drawings, photographs, school reports, awards, certificates, medals, and in fact any other mementos to remember those special years at school. The book can be divided into sections for each year.

If you design your own cross-stitch panel for the cover you can include personal memories about your child's past, and relevant smaller motifs can be worked and attached to the envelopes.

YOU WILL NEED

- ***A book of blank pages to cover***
- ***Manilla envelopes the same size as (or smaller than) the book pages***
- ***Gingham fabric***
- ***Even-weave fabric (16-count Aida cloth was used here)***
- ***Stranded floss and tapestry needle***
- ***Embroidery frame (optional)***
- ***Pins***
- ***Fusible webbing***

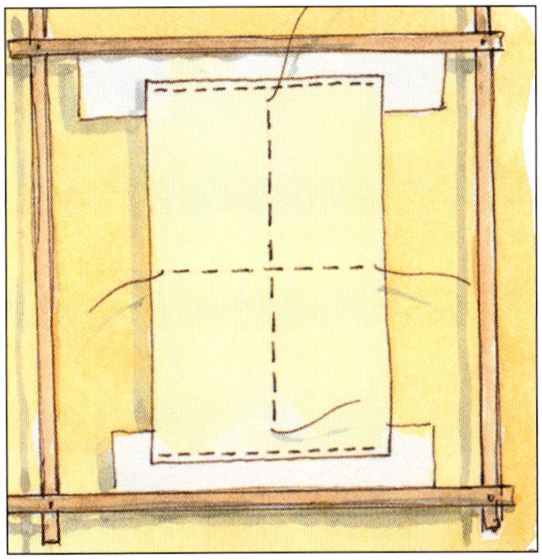

1 Decide on the size of the cross-stitch panel and allow an extra 2 in. (5 cm) all around. Cut out the even-weave fabric and attach it to a frame if desired. Mark the horizontal and vertical centers of the fabric with colored basting thread. Always calculate the position of motifs and borders from the center.

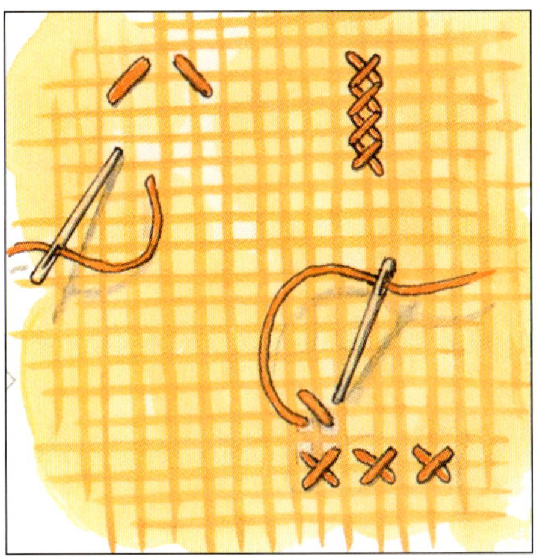

2 Design your own map or street plan, or perhaps choose another motif, and draw the outlines on squared graph paper, allowing one square for each cross stitch.

3 Following the chart, work the cross-stitch panel, sewing two strands of floss if you are using Aida cloth. One square represents one cross stitch. To give the best effect, the top stitch should always be worked in the same direction.

4 When the stitching is complete, cut the panel to size, leaving enough fabric to pull a few strands away gently to make the fringe.

5 To cover the book, cut the gingham to fit, allowing an extra 2 in. (5 cm) all around. Iron the fabric flat before starting.

Remove a couple of pages from your book to allow for the bulk of each envelope. Use fusible webbing to attach the cross-stitch panel and motifs.

6 Fit the cover around the book, wrong side out. Pin and baste it to fit, making sure the seam allowance on the inside flap is correct. Remove the cover and backstitch or machine stitch the seams across the flaps.

7 Turn right side out and make sure the corners are square and neat. Fit the cover on the book, turning the seam allowance toward the outside of the cover to give the spine a good edge. Cut a piece of fusible webbing to the size of your motifs and iron the stitched motifs to the front as desired.

8 Attach the envelopes to the pages, using two-sided tape. These will be useful to hold school report cards and certificates. Don't make the envelopes too bulky or they will pull away from their backing.

MEMORY BOXES

Anyone who has ever filled a shoe box with family photographs or crammed small treasures into a cigar box has already made a memory box. This section gives you the very basics on how to make your own memory box to keep your favourite memorabilia—letters, seashells, report cards, broken pieces of jewelry, snippets of baby hair, and all of the ephemera of belonging. However varied the design, most boxes share the same basic architectural elements—a case, a tray, a lid, and a flap. But the number of ways we decorate these boxes is endless, making each one a unique object of beauty.

The Basics

There is a very comforting repetitive quality to the steps involved in making boxes. In the beginning you will probably keep referring to these pages, but very soon you will not even need to peek at them to create your own beautiful boxes.

PARTS OF THE BOX

A box is composed of several separate units—the case, the flaps, the tray, and the lid. The case, consisting of a front, spine and back, is constructed by assembling the boards on the covering material, often leaving a space between the boards (called a *joint*) to act as a hinge.

The most basic box is a simple case with no flaps, no trays, and no lid.

Flaps are panels attached to the case at the top (head), bottom (tail), and side (fore-edge). They can be made separately and glued on the case or they can grow from the case itself. Flaps keep the contents of the box from falling out.

Trays consist of base boards with walls glued to them prior to covering. Trays are three-walled or four-walled, depending on the style of box.

Lids, either freestanding or attached to the spine, are panels built to extend slightly beyond the parameters of a tray. They create a lip for easy accessibility and lifting and are often embellished with knobs, buttons, ribbons, and other fasteners.

GRAIN DIRECTION

Anyone who has ever torn an article out of a newsprint has had a lesson in grain direction. Pulled in one direction, the paper tears beautifully, but when pulled in the perpendicular direction, the paper rips jaggedly. The clean tear is with the grain, the ragged one, against the grain.

Grain is inherent in paper, cloth and board. It is determined by an alignment of fibers. The direction in which most of the fibers are aligned is the grain direction of the material.

For the movable parts of a box to work easily and without stress, the grain must run parallel to this hinging action. In a book, grain runs parallel to its spine, making it easy to turn the pages and manipulate the cover. The same is true in boxmaking; the grain must run parallel to the spine of the box.

HOW TO DETERMINE GRAIN

The best way to determine grain is through your sense of touch. For paper and cloth, gently bend (don't crease) the material and roll it back and forth several times. Let the paper or cloth relax, then bend and roll it in the opposite direction. The direction in which you feel the least resistance is the grain direction.

For board, hold a corner in both hands and flex it, then release the board. Flex the board in the opposite direction. The flexing direction of least resistance is the grain direction.

MEASURING

All boxes start from the inside out. The first piece of board to be measured and cut is the base board, the piece on which your objects (books, photos, marbles) will sit. All of the other boards take their measurements from the base. The base has two dimensions—height and width.

Height is the distance from top to bottom or, in the bookbinder's language (used throughout this book), from head to tail. Width is the distance from side to side or, more precisely, from spine to fore-edge. The third dimension of the box, its depth, is found in its walls. Depth refers to the thickness of the object to be boxed; the distance, for example, from the top card to the bottom card in a deck of cards.

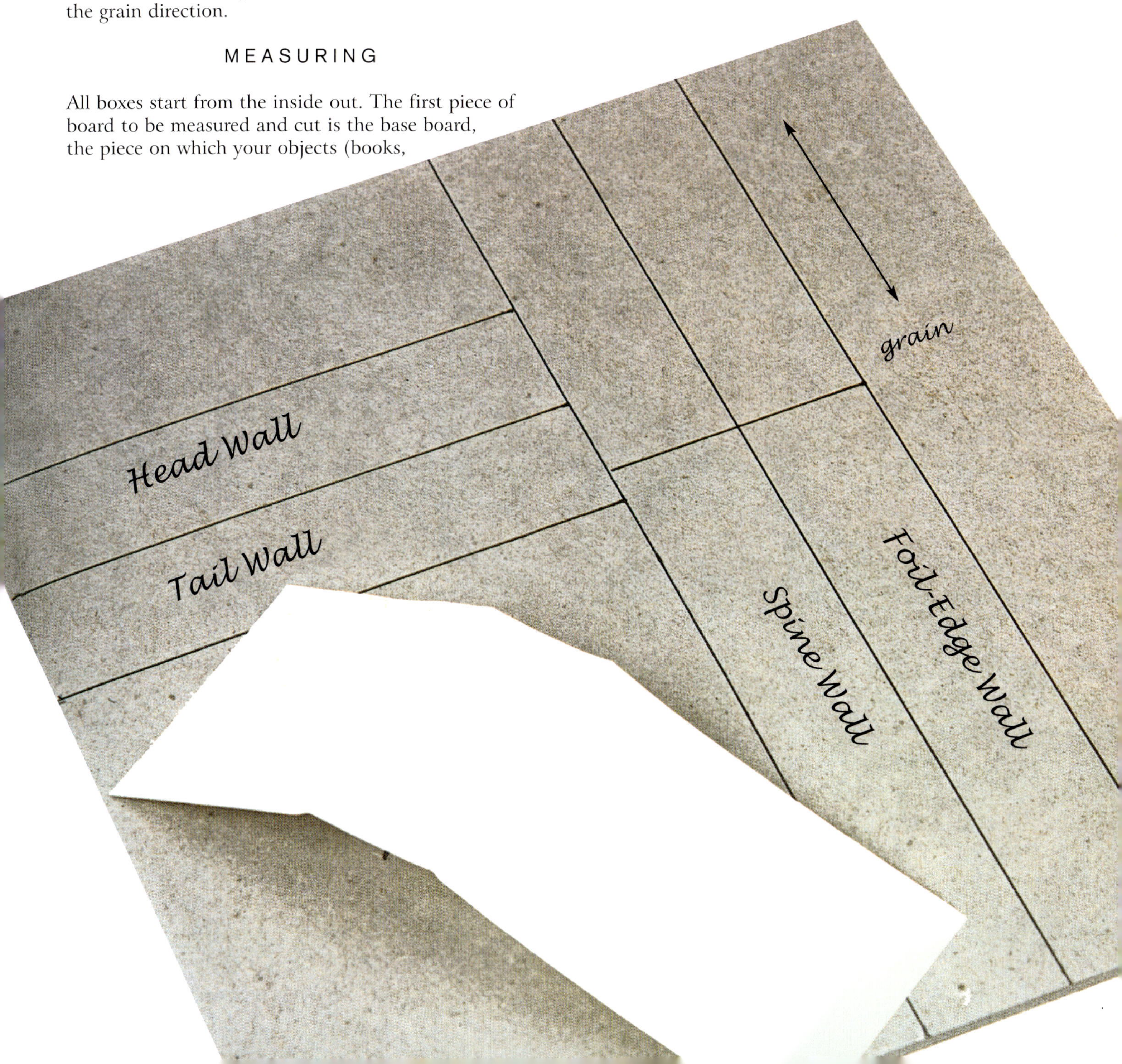

CUTTING

A wonderful piece of equipment to have to hand is a paper cutter. Whether tabletop or freestanding, a paper cutter (or the more substantial board shears) makes the difference between easy and laborious cutting. A good cutter that has a bed with a true edge perpendicular to the cutting edge, a clamp to hold the material in place, and a pair of sharp upper and lower knives is a joy to use. If a cutter is not available, use a utility knife and a T-square.

To make sure accuracy in cutting, you must follow a four-step process.

1 Determine grain direction of the board. (Review Grain Direction on page 210 if you need help with this.) Grain direction must run from head to tail on all boards.

2 Rough cut the board to the approximate size needed for the box. An oversized board is difficult to handle and will not fit on a tabletop paper cutter.

3 Square the board by trimming one long edge of board and a perpendicular short edge to form a true right angle.

4 Mark the board by placing the object to be boxed on the squared corner and making pencilled markings of desired height and width.

To determine the depth of the object to be boxed, crease a scrap of paper to form a right angle; slide this scrap under the object and make a parallel crease in the scrap paper, snugly enclosing the object within these two creases. Transfer this measurement—the distance from one crease to the other—to your board.

HOW TO CONSTRUCT THE TRAY

G-clamp a wooden board onto your tabletop. Set down a piece of wax paper. Place the base board on the wax paper. Using full-strength PVA and a small brush, paint a thin line of glue along the edge of the head wall where it touches the base. Position this wall against the clamped wooden board and push the base against it. (The clamped board supports the wall and helps to maintain a right angle.) Wipe away excess glue with your bone folder. Glue the fore-edge wall, painting the glue along the edge touching the base and also along the edge that meets the head wall. Glue the tail wall, painting the glue along the edge touching the base and also along the edge that meets the fore-edge wall. Glue the spine wall, painting the glue along the edge touching the base and also along the two edges that meet the head and tail walls. Let the tray set until it is dry (15 minutes). Peel the tray off the wax paper, and sand any rough joints. The tray is now ready for covering.

COVERING THE OUTSIDE

Cut a piece of paper long enough to wrap around all walls, plus ½ in. (1 cm). (If your decorative paper is not long enough, use two shorter pieces; plan the seam to fall at a corner.) In width, the paper should be twice the depth of the tray, plus 1½ in. (4 cm).

Paste out the paper. Give the paper time to relax and uncurl. Position your tray, with the bottom of the tray facing you, approximately ¾ in. (2 cm) away from the long edge of the paper and ½ in. (1 cm) away from the short edge. Crease the ½ in. (1 cm) extension around the corner and onto the wall.

Roll the tray on the paper, pushing the tray snugly into each right angle as it is formed. Before making the final roll, check the paper for stretch. If the paper has stretched beyond the board edge, trim it to fit. Remember, wet paper tends to tear. To minimize this risk, place a piece of wax paper on top of the paper to be trimmed, and cut through the wax paper, using a sawing motion with your knife. Use a bone folder to crease the ¾ in. (2 cm) turn-ins onto the bottom of the tray. Clip the corners with scissors, and press the paper into position.

FINISHING THE INSIDE

To finish the inside of the tray (A), slivers of paper exactly one board thickness in width must be removed at each of the four corners. Position the tray on its spine wall, on a cutting mat. Place your metal triangle on the paper. One edge of the triangle should touch the board edge (thickness) while the triangle is slid firmly into the curve of the wrapped paper in the left-hand corner. With your knife, cut through the paper. Start the cut with the tip of the knife actually touching the board. Make a parallel cut, one board thickness away from the original cut. Important: Do not start this cut at the board. With the triangle repositioned, place the knife 1½ board thicknesses away from the board, and cut. With your knife, make a diagonal cut between the starting points of these two parallel cuts. This cut releases the sliver of paper—one board thickness in width—which allows the covering paper to be turned neatly into the inside of the tray. It also creates a mitered corner. Keeping the tray resting on its spine wall, repeat these cuts in the right-hand corner.

Turn the tray onto its fore-edge wall. Make the cuts, as described previously, in first the left and then the right-hand corners.

Note: These cuts are made in only two of the tray's four walls. I pick the other pair of opposites, the head and tail walls.

Your final cuts are made with scissors. Push the spine wall covering into the tray, pressing it against the inside wall and forcing the paper into the right-angle where the base meets the spine wall. Gently crease the paper by running your bone folder along this seam. Pull the paper back to the outside and cut away the two corners, removing 45° triangles of paper. Make sure the cuts stop at the crease mark made in the previous step. Repeat with the fore-edge wall.

You are now ready to paste (B). Starting with the head, paste out the covering paper and push it to the inside, pressing it sharply into all seams. Rub with your bone folder to eliminate air bubbles and paste lumps. Repeat at the tail. (Since these two wall coverings have not had slivers of paper removed from them, they overlap the corners. This makes sure that the cardboard seam will be covered.) Paste out the spine wall covering and press into place. Paste out the fore-edge wall covering and press into place (C).

A

B

C

Book-in-a-Box

This bright and cheerful book-in-a-box can be used to keep your memory book in a special place, as well as giving you a handy spot to store your craft equipment. Collage the outside of your box with bright paper designs and matching tissue paper. Pick out a bold pattern to create a theme.

YOU WILL NEED

Matt board (mounting card)

Sheet of colorful giftwrap paper with a bold design

Sheets of colored tissue paper

Acrylic paint

Ribbon

Bead (optional)

A5 hardback blank book or scrapbook

Gummed brown paper tape

Masking tape

Cutting mat

1 Measure an A5 book and cut a piece of mat board (mounting card) to make the tray. Leave approximately ¾ in. (2 cm) all around for the sides of the tray. Cut the matt board part way through at the fold lines and cut along lines A to create flaps. Turn the flaps in and secure them with masking tape. Repeat to make the box, approximately 3½ in. (9 cm) deep, using the tray as a guide to its length and width.

2 Form the shelf for the tray to sit on by cutting four pieces of mat board 2¼ x 8¾ in. (5.5 x 22.5 cm). Hold two pieces together with masking tape and tape them to the inside of the box to form one side of the shelf. Repeat on the other side.

3 To make the lid, cut two pieces of mat board using the measurements of the box. Tape the pieces together and attach along the back of the box. Make a small loop from ribbon and attach it to the center of the lid between the two pieces of board. Secure the loop in place with tape. If you wish, you can attach a bead or button to the front of the box to fasten the loop over. Make a small loop for the tray and attach it to the center front of the tray with tape.

4 Apply gummed brown paper tape all over the box and the inside of the tray to make a neat surface. Apply decoupage or collage to the outside and inside of the box, and the inside of the tray. If you are using fine tissue paper, you may first want to paint the gummed brown paper tape with white acrylic to enhance colors. Finish the box by cutting out bold, colorful designs, and glueing them to the lid, tray, and inside of the box. You can use motifs that echo the patterns and colors on the box to decorate the pages of your book. Paint the outside of the tray in a bright color.

This scrapbook is also the ideal place to store items that you might want to display in future memory books. Underneath the snug-fitting tray, you will have plenty of room for scissors, glue, craft knife, and the other supplies you will need to make more scrapbooks.

Trinket Box

This brightly colored trinket box shows that decorating objects with collage can be a fun way to make a highly individual gift.

MAKING THE BOX

1 Cut three pieces of corrugated cardboard 4¾ in. (12 cm) square and two pieces 4¼ x 4¾ in. (11 x 12 cm). Tear eight pieces of brown paper tape 4 in. (10 cm) long. Using a damp sponge, apply water to the shiny side of the tape. Use one of the large squares as the base. Tape the other pieces to the base to form a cross with pieces of cardboard of equal size opposite each other. Lift each side of the box to a vertical position and tape the corners. Rub the tape until smooth, being careful not to push in the sides of the box.

2 To make the lid cut one 4¾ in. (12 cm) square and one 4¼ in. (11 cm) square from a sheet of corrugated cardboard. Cut 4 triangles with the height and base both measuring 4½ in. (11.5 cm). Using gum strip (brown paper tape), attach the smaller square to the top of the larger one.

3 Turn the squares over so that the smaller of the two is face down. Tape the triangles to the base. Lift up the triangles to form a pyramid and tape along each adjoining edge. Cover the pyramid with layers of pasted paper and leave to dry for several days.

4 Tear the dark blue purchased or handmade paper into strips ¾ x 5½ in. (1.5 x 14 cm). Brush glue, diluted with water to a milky consistency, onto the box. Apply the strips of paper. Carefully glue one end over the edge and the other end onto the base.

5 Cover the four sides of the box with strips and torn shapes. Paste under and over each piece of paper. Decorate the box using the same technique. You may want to collage the base and inside of the box, too.

6 To make the feet cut two bottle corks in half. This is quite tricky; always take great care when using craft knives. Cut a third cork in half to use as a knob on the top of the lid. Cut or sand it to a ball shape and add an indent, to about half its depth, in one place, so that the ball will sit on top of the pyramid.

8 Mix epoxy resin according to the manufacturer's instructions. Apply it to the uncovered end of each cork and position one at each corner of the base of the box. Apply glue to the top point of the lid and press on the indented cork. When the glue is dry, seal the box using a water-based varnish.

7 Tear a strip of paper slightly longer and wider than the cork. Brush the paper with undiluted glue and wrap it around the cork. Cover one end of each half-cork with a circle of pasted paper.

BELOW: *Here is another idea for a trinket box using a wonderful mixture of buttons and leftover lengths of ribbon.*

Glossary

Awl
Pointed metal implement with wooden handles, useful for making preparatory holes through layers of paper, card stock, or cardboard.

Batten
A long flat strip of wood.

Batting
Layers or sheets of raw cotton, wool, or synthetic fibrous material used for lining quilts or for stuffing or packaging.

Beating
The process of macerating plant fibers in order to break them down into pulp for the purpose of sheet formation. This may be done mechanically or by hand.

Bias tape
A narrow strip of cloth cut on the bias, folded, and used for finishing or decorating clothing.

Bleeding
The spreading out of ink or paint on paper which has not been sized.

Boards
Hard covers, covered with paper or cloth, to create the solid front and back covers of a book.

Bonding
The interaction between cellulose fibers and water which, when beaten and dried, adhere to form paper.

Bone folder
A tool made from a smooth, lozenge-shaped piece of bone. It is used to make folds in paper and card stock, or for smoothing out creases and air bubbles in pasted lining paper.

Bookcloth
Paper-backed fabric used for book covers.

Bookcloth tape
Tape backed with adhesive, used to cover a book spine or bind cover borders.

Brayer
A printer's hand-inking roller.

Couching
In papermaking, the process of transferring a freshly made sheet of paper from the mold surface onto a dampened felt.

Deckle
In papermaking, the removable frame which rests on top of the mold to hold the pulp and define the edge of the sheet.

Deckle-edge scissors
Scissors with blades for making a deckle-edged cut, such as a scalloped edge.

Dowel rod
A headless peg of wood, metal, or plastic for holding together components of a structure.

Duct tape
A wide, silvery, cloth adhesive tape.

Dyes
Soluble coloring agents that penetrate the actual structure of a fiber, and cling to it.

Embedding
Incorporating a decorative element into a sheet of paper during sheet formation.

Embossing
The process of creating a raised or depressed design from a surface.

Embossing liquid
Liquid used to add a three-dimensional quality to a page or cover.

Endpaper
A folded sheet, one leaf of which is pasted to the front or back of a hardcover book. The other leaf is pasted to the first or last page of the book.

Fabric photo
A photo that has been transferred onto fabric, usually cotton.

Felt
In papermaking, the woven woollen blanket onto which a newly formed sheet of paper is transferred or couched. Also a type of thick soft cloth made from a pressed mass of wool and hair.

Fiber
The fine, thread-like filaments in plant tissue used to make pulp for papermaking.

Glue
Pliable adhesives used on the backs of many bindings; these are archival and easily removed.

Hemp
A bast fiber plant (*Cannabis sativa*) of high cellulose content. The fiber extracted from the stem is used to make rope and tough fabrics.

Iron-on interfacing
Double-sided tape or fabric with adhesive, ironed on to strengthen and stiffen fabric.

Leather punch
A rotating punch, used for making holes in stiff or thick materials.

Marbling
Creating decorative papers with a marble-like pattern by floating color on the surface and transferring the pattern onto paper.

Mitering
The process of finishing the corners of a book.

Mold
A rectangular wooden frame covered with a sieve-like laid or woven wire surface, used for sheet-forming in papermaking.

Papier mâché
The French for "chewed paper." A material made of pulped paper mixed with glue that can be molded when moist, and then baked to produce a strong but light substance that can be painted and polished.

Paste
Adhesives made from wheat or rice flour, used to stick leather to spines, paper to paper, and paper to boards.

Photographic mounting spray
Type of adhesive glue used to paste photographs into scrapbooks.

Pinking shears
Shears with a saw-toothed inner edge on the blades for making a zigzag cut.

Polyboard (also foam board or foam core)
Foam sandwiched between two pieces of cardboard, frequently used for the covers of books.

Post
A stack of newly formed paper sheets alternated with couching felts, ready for pressing.

Post bound scrapbook
A scrapbook containing punched pages held together by metal posts.

Pressing
In papermaking, the process of pressing paper to remove as much water as possible before drying, and to help bond the fibers into a strong sheet.

Raffia
The fiber from the leaves of a Madagascar palm tree, *Raphia ruffia*, used for cloths, hats, and baskets.

Shim
A thin often tapered piece of material (wood, metal, or stone) used to fill in space between things (as for support, leveling, adjustment of fit).

Sizing
The process of adding a starch or gelatine solution (a "size") to pulp or paper to decrease the paper's absorbency.

Vat
Container for pulp in which sheets of paper are made.

Vellum
A writing surface derived from the skin of stillborn or newborn calves or lambs.

Webbing
Strong, narrow, closely woven fabric.

White glue
A pliable, plastic-based adhesive; it is non-archival.

Index